T0166061

# Resident Deputy Sheriff

in
## Wild and Woolly West Marin
## 1964 to 1969
### *… and then some !*

**San Geronimo Valley, view from Moon Hill,
my primary beat for five years.**

## A collection of vivid vignettes by
# Weldon C. Travis
### Compassionate Adventurer ™

Order this book online at www.trafford.com
or email orders@trafford.com

Most Trafford titles are also available at major online book retailers.

Author Credits: Harry Koch; Richard Gill

Printed in the United States of America.

ISBN: 978-1-4669-0028-8 (sc)
ISBN: 978-1-4669-0030-1 (hc)
ISBN: 978-1-4669-0029-5 (e)

Library of Congress Control Number: 2012902949

*Trafford rev. 04/05/2012*

www.trafford.com

North America & international
toll-free: 1 888 232 4444 (USA & Canada)
phone: 250 383 6864 ♦ fax: 812 355 4082

# Table of Contents

# Foreword

I was your personal cop, your keeper of the peace, your friend, the one you called when you needed someone and didn't have anyone else more appropriate, or handy, to call or didn't know whom to call; the one who patched you up to keep you from bleeding to death before you got to the hospital, the one who took you to jail or the nut ward when you really needed to go; the one who forestalled or maybe prevented your suicide; the one who tried to wash the bloodstains off your rug or blankets; he who tenaciously, surreptitiously investigated you as a homicide suspect while consoling you over the sudden, unexplained death of your toddler in her sleep; the one who subdued you in your violent paranoia when you were crazed with angel dust; the man you invited to your college graduation after you straightened out your life; the one who drank, reminisced, laughed, suffered with you, rejoiced in your first live-born baby after being there at your sad miscarriages; the one who pursued you at high speed, impounded your car and took you to juvie hall to give you time to think and maybe keep you from killing yourself and your young friends; the one who squeezed your carotid artery shut so your mother could thank me later; the one you supported in **my** times of need.

This is my story for you, so you can better know me as I so intimately knew you. It's only fair, is it not? They are little tales of happiness and sadness, accomplishment and disappointment, silliness and sobriety, stupidity and enlightenment, risk and loss, raging fear and reluctant courage, exhilaration in the knowledge of having done, I think, the right or necessary things most of the time. Most took place during the late sixties and early seventies in "Marvelous Marin" County, just North of the Golden Gate Bridge when I was a Resident Deputy Sheriff in the San Geronimo Valley and the rest of West Marin. Things, they were a-happening—being fired and reinstated (see post-

Epilogue), the Vietnam War, crazy days (daze?) in the Haight-Ashbury, Janis and Jerry and Naomi and Sly, shoot-out at the Civic Center. Day or night, when you called, I came, whether you wanted me or not.

You are my Friend and Compatriot. You stood beside me when I was troubled by the bad things I've seen and had to do—the blood and guts and the gore. When I was hurting deep inside—when I needed you, you were there. Other times I was there for you in your own time of need, like when your child died from SIDS and you had to shoot up some heroin before you allowed me in, or when your spouse abandoned you when most needed. Do you remember? I do—and I am thankful and grateful for our friendship. I open myself to you as you have exposed yourself to me. Treat me gently; I already have a lot of hurts.

# Acknowledgements

My wife, the beautiful and talented "Serene Irene, the Bawdy House Queen," who has stood by me and lain by my side for eleven years. She knows the troubles I've seen and continue to have on occasion. She's an artist, former beauty queen and model, and has helped me tremendously in this production by not only proof-reading but also by her gentle critiquing of contents.

My daughter, Katrina Lara, a "wise old soul" from infancy, who always has had faith in me. "You're never too old to learn nor ever too young to teach."

Russ Hunt, my primary partner and relief Deputy in the early days. He saved my butt a couple of times; retired as a Lieutenant and still lives in West Marin.

Paul Fontana, modern day word wrangling wizard.

Bill Gleason for his back cover recommendation. He's a local friend and fellow club member, retired homicide investigator with the Los Angeles Sheriff's Department after having served 27 years. He caused the arrest of Charles Manson and others who were later identified as being responsible for the murders of actress Sharon Tate and six others in 1969. He also investigated many other major homicide cases during his career. As a continuing public service, he investigates missing children cases for the National Center for Missing and Exploited Children at no cost other than expenses.

Ernest Hemingway, for his harsh yet tender succinctness and who knew "For Whom the Bell Tolls." Suicide is selfish and leaves the survivors to grieve.

Fritz Perls, Gestalt psychotherapist who suggested that "The whole is different from the sum of its parts."

Dr. and U. S. Senator Sam Ichiye Hayakawa, semanticist, counter-revolutionary and former President of San Francisco State University, drove a Jaguar X-12 and wore a tam o'shanter, who helped us Peace Officers and law enforcement folks to better understand through accurate communication and perceptions the varied composition of the populace whose needs we serve.

My martial arts sifus and senseis—for the wisdom and survival skills they imparted in a variety of disciplines.

My Native American friends, who taught me how to read track, reconstruct events, sense danger, prepared me to kill or to die honorably; who reinforced my connectedness to Mother Earth.

# No Mea Culpa*

This is **mostly** autobiographical in the sense that I'm sharing my life with you. These are happenings in which I was immersed, screw-ups and all. If I were not personally on the scene of these little vignettes, they are as best that I can recall them being told to me by persons whose integrity and honesty I have grown to trust and, indeed on some occasions, literally bet my life on. That trust paid off, as you can see, since I'm still here.

I've filled in some of the blanks, presumed some of the dialogue, quoted as best I remember, made some up when I wasn't sure. It's been a few years and a lot of Tennessee sour mash bourbon, too much of the latter, actually, and not enough of the former. Those incidents that may be offensive or discomforting to the guilty are not meant to be embarrassing to you or your offspring at this late date, so I've altered some names, locations and times and I hope you won't sue me for defamation of character. It's been quite a ride and I hope you can reflect back with me and enjoy it, too. Those of you who haven't yet gotten over it deserve to live in your own Hell. And to you younger readers: look upon this as a small piece of local history.

**\* I am not to be blamed**

# Cop on the beat

There stands the Cop on the beat
Set apart by his badge and his gun.
To some he's a hero with flat feet
Yet he's called a pig by the young.

Just a man with a job to do,
Keeping the peace for me and you.
Sometimes we feel outrage
When we're caught on the other side.
Still, we have nothing to fear
If we have nothing to hide.

Long is the night of the patrolman's road
And many the problems he'll face.
Is it any wonder his feelings get cold
When dealing with the human race?

Ask the child who is lost from his home
And returned by the man in blue.
"What do you say to the policeman, dear?"
He'll say it for us . . . "Thank you."

Richard Gill, Roving Poet of Rough And Ready California, 1974

One of my many friends—a sculptor/welder of copper figures very large and smaller; a philosopher who has traveled across our country with his Medicine Man wagon, creatively encouraging us to explore a kinder, more gentle way of treating each other and Mother Earth. His philosophy: Dream, Think, Believe, Dare! It's the way I've lived, too.

# A Part of America Died

## By Harry Koch

Somebody killed a policeman today,
And a part of America died.
A piece of our country he swore to protect,
Will be buried with him at his side.

The suspect who shot him will stand up in court,
With counsel demanding his rights,
While a young widowed mother must work for her kids,
And spend alone many long nights.

The beat that he walked was a battlefield, too,
Just as if he'd gone off to war.
Though the flag of our nation won't fly at half mast,
To his name they will add a gold star.

Yes, somebody killed a policeman today,
It happened in your town or mine.
While we slept in comfort behind our locked doors,
A cop put his life on the line.

Now, his ghost walks a beat on a dark city street,
And he stands at each new rookie's side.
He answered the call and gave us his all,
And a part of America died.

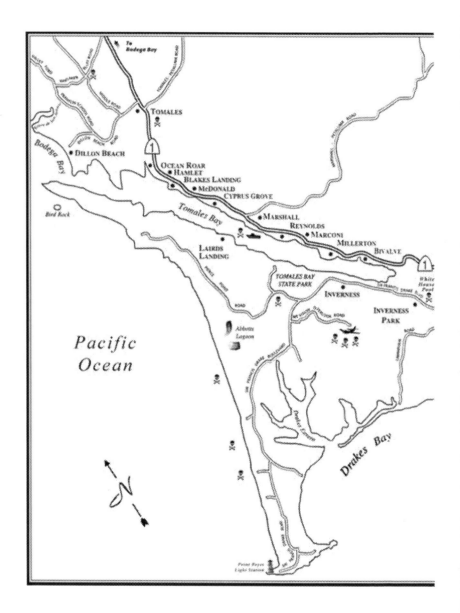

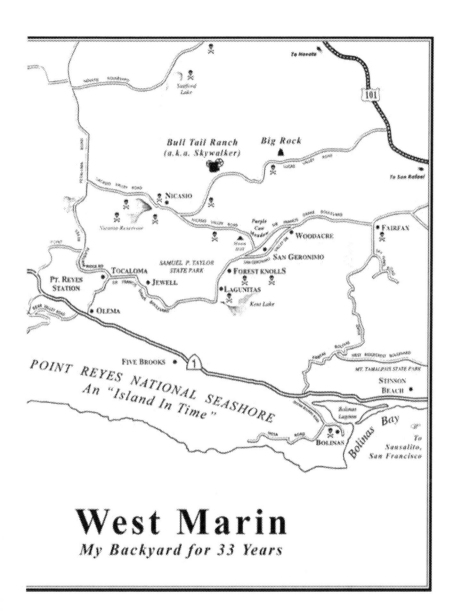

# West Marin
*My Backyard for 33 Years*

# Twelve-fingered Marshall

I was a rookie, working the dayshift in the old County Jail in the basement of the Marin County Court House, built around the turn of the century, since burned down by an arsonist. The elevator shaft was now where the gallows had been. The condemned were dropped down from a trap door on the court floor into the Sheriff's Department. Convenient and efficient.

A heavy-set guy in plain clothes waddled down the corridor from the parking lot and said he was there to pick up one of our inmates. So'kay—"Could you show me the warrant and your identification?"

He plopped down a huge hand on the booking counter. I looked in amazement: he had a thumb and FIVE perfectly proportioned fingers. It took a few seconds to recover my newly acquired authority. I told him that I really need more identification before I could release the inmate into his custody. He plopped down his other hand. Same thing. This guy had TWELVE digits on his hands. I wonder what he had in his shoes!

He showed me the warrant and off they went. Weird!

Chief Jailer Lt. Duke Snyder told me later that, not long before my time, a Texas Ranger had picked up an inmate for extradition back to his home state. Duke said that he and the Ranger took care of all the paperwork then brought the poor guy out for the change of custody. The Ranger introduced himself, asked the inmate his name, then cold-cocked him and picked him up, just to let him know where they stood. He understood—no hard feelings. They went out to the Ranger's open flatbed truck where the inmate was shackled to a large O-ring in the center of the truck and off they went, back to Texas. Must have been one Hell of a long ride home . . .

That beat up old booking counter, if it could talk, would have some interesting tales. One guy high on drugs lunged over

1

it at me one night. My ribs had been separated in a beef and I was hurting pretty bad. Another deputy rabbit-chopped him on the back of his neck and Sgt. Wade Powell uppercut him in the solar plexus. He went down like a sack of cement.

# Billy Wallace, Texas Ranger

Billy was big and soft, Irish with a fair complexion, red hair and freckles, a quick, high, almost falsetto laugh and smooth hands. He was tired of being on-call as a Resident Deputy in West Marin. Basically, we couldn't leave our beats for five days running unless we had a subpoena for Court. We even took our cars in for service on our days off, unless the tires got so bald we risked a high-speed blowout. He'd worked and lived out on the Coast, mostly in Stinson Beach and Bolinas, the town that won't be found, then was re-assigned to The Valley beat where he had moved to Woodacre to get away from the fog. He wasn't a happy camper. He didn't last in The Valley very long, but that was to my advantage.

I had been working as a rookie in the Jail for only a few months and had told Captain Carl Seares that I very much wanted to be a Resident Deputy out in West Marin. As a kid, I used to be the good cowboy or sheriff: Red Ryder riding the rimrock; Roy Rogers without his yucky girlfriend, Dale; Bat Masterson or Wyatt Earp. Gene Autry was too much of a goody-two-shoes for me. Once in a while I'd give in and be Frank James or Cole Younger, but not for long. I always won the fistfights and gun battles when I couldn't talk the hard-riding outlaws, who always needed a shave, into Jail. My six-shooter cap guns had genuine pearl handled longhorn steer grips and I wore them low for a smooth-'n'-easy fast draw. When I moved to Woodacre after high school, I got a job on Ralph Roy's dairy ranch, which is now the San Geronimo Valley Golf Course. Later, Jack Dougan had me feeding his cows in Nicasio where I tried bulldogging a heifer in the slop around the outside hayracks. What a mess I was! Jack took a high-pressure water hose to wash off all the mud and manure, laughing all the time. I'd never tasted cow shit before. I didn't care for it. Later I did a little recreational bareback bronc riding in local rodeos. Got busted up the last time I rode at thirty-seven, just to show my five-year-old son, Zachary, what I used to do for fun. He was more worried that the clown had my Stetson than he was about my broken ribs.

I really wanted to live that role now. Nowadays, we call it "creative visualization" but, by damn, I **made** it happen. Billy and I had gotten our State-mandated basic training out of the way up in Santa Rosa a while back (what a hellish five weeks that was—another tale, but I got to know Billy and Russ and Gary pretty well). Billy had seen action as a door gunner in an Army Huey in some place called Cambodia before he'd come to the S/O, or I'd even *heard* of Vietnam. He wouldn't tell me anymore, in fact he shouldn't have told me that much, because **we weren't even over there then**. I agreed not to share . . . later my brother-in-law bought the farm at Khe Sahn during the 1968 Tet Offensive and I was pissed with myself for not questioning further.

Billy told me that he had a new girlfriend with really nice tits and they were sparkin' down at the base of the Nicasio Reservoir spillway (really out of the way, where they wouldn't be bothered). They were getting pretty friendly, might call it frisky, when she felt his off-duty snub-nose .38 on his waist.

"That's it—take me home."

"Why, what's wrong with me having a gun?"

"Because you're either a cop or a gangster and, either way, I don't want anything to do with you."

Billy really wanted to go back to Texas, back to his roots where he fit in better, kind of like his Tony Llama boots that were so well broken in. He wanted to become a Texas Ranger, just as I had wished I were born a Red Ryder and had a half-breed kid brother named Li'l Beaver.

The Captain called me in one day and asked if I still wanted the job. I jumped at it. He told me I had one week to find a place to live and move on to the beat. Marylu Z. Giddings, the Woodacre Postmaster, was suggested to me as good resource for housing (and other community knowledge). Within a day, she had me set up in a triplex on Central Avenue, a main road in to Woodacre. Not much privacy and anyone who wanted to know if was home or on the prowl had only to drive by to check for my patrol car. Some times, I'd leave the patrol car in the driveway and take a large portable radio in my own car, just to keep 'em guessing. Never thought about the liability factor . . . and my Sergeant didn't know what I was doing most of the time. He DID like my results, though, a 97% conviction rate over the five years I worked for him.

Billy told me to meet him at his place at eight o'clock on the next Friday morning so he could break me in, show me the beat. I got there right on the dot, my brass and boots all shined up, a fresh uniform, briefcase and clipboard, hideout derringer—I was ready! We piled into his beat-up 1963 Plymouth patrol car. I'd started for the passenger side but he said, "You drive, I parked this thing two nights ago, it's got exactly 100,000 miles on it, it's shot and dangerous to drive and I'm not driving it one more mile." "So that's the way it's going to be," I said to myself.

We went down to the Firehouse to gas up, then out to Pt. Reyes Station where the old firehouse and substation were and where I met some of the guys I'd be working with. Sergeant Bertrand gave me a few guidelines about getting reports in on time, staying on my beat pretty much, keeping my nose clean, where to log in warrants, civil papers and vacation checks. Then to the firehouses in Stinson Beach, Bolinas and Hick's Valley. I noticed that the front end shimmied a lot and the car tended to drift all over the road if we got over sixty five. Billy must have really been hard on it, or had not taken care of it very well. Now I knew all the places where I could write my reports in safety and comfort, grab some coffee or take a leak. "That's it, take me home, it's all yours."

That's it?? Nothing about bad guys, back roads, shortcuts? Nope, "It's all yours." Four hours, four firehouses, maybe 65 miles, that was **it**! Then I realized I could make of it what I wanted, make it my Valley, my towns, my people—I was

5

the new sheriff, a young Gary Cooper with High Noon coming on. It was just fine and my shirt fit just a little tighter.

Billy started working "over the Hill" out of the main office in San Rafael and we kind of faded away from each other.

Once or twice I asked him about some kid or some crook, or where to find one of the seven Dolcini ranches.

A few months later, Billy went back to Texas—Plano, I think.

Billy was a Texas Ranger, last I knew . . .

# Sledgehammer Mechanic vs. Red Buick Convertible

Don Yerion ran the Forest Knolls Garage, beer bar and trailer park, with his folks keeping an eye on him and the businesses. He was a tall, lanky, good-natured guy who would help any fellow or gal down on their luck. He was also a ham-fisted, one-punch brawler—that's usually all it took, for one or several at a time.

In another chapter, I might tell you about him breaking a bad guy's jaw in three places with one mighty punch; or manhandling a 55 gallon barrel of kerosene that screwed up his back in a major way.

He'd raise Hell on occasion with his good buddy, Dean de la Montana, who owned the Oak Tree Inn in San Geronimo down Sir Francis Drake Highway.

One sunny mid-morning, Dean pulled up in his shiny red '56 Buick convertible (with the top down) across the road from the service station. Some poor fool was pumping his own gas when Dean broke out his .44 Magnum S&W revolver and shouted out, "God damn you, Yerion, I told you to stay away from my wife!" He then cut loose with all six rounds over the top of the station into the safe hillside beyond, then sped off.

That poor soul pumping gasoline jumped into his car and peeled out, taking the pump nozzle with him and leaving the ruptured hose pouring gasoline all around the pump island. He never came back to pay.

The next morning, Dean pulled up to the same spot and hollered out to Don and, with his deep guffaw. "I sure got you good, didn't I?"

Well, it just so happened that Don kept a Ruger .44 Magnum semi-automatic carbine in the shop. Turnabout is fair play, right? A dozen or so rounds later, Dean left in a huff and a hurry and didn't return for quite a few days after that.

* * *

## The Gypsy Jokers vs. the Hell's Angels

Don drove a tank in Korea, in '53 I think, but he didn't talk much about it, like most vets who've seen Hell prematurely. Some nights, he'd hang out at the station, tinkering or hammering away or "holding court" with friends. If he'd had too much to drink, he'd walk home, a half mile or so away.

Now, the Gypsy Jokers and the Hell's Angels both claimed the Forest Knolls Lodge as their own turf. One gang was inside (I can't remember which) and the other was in the shadows near Papermill Creek. They were trying to figure out how to operate a .30 caliber, air-cooled machine gun, one familiar to Don.

"Give me that damned thing," Don grumbled disgustedly. Locked and loaded, he cut loose with several bursts into the general area above the tavern. All of the chopped Harleys roared off into the night like a bevy of quail.

I miss the old poop . . .

That same machine gun had been set up to ambush me one night. I usually made it a point to cover every single road on my beat each 24-hour day but, that night, I missed that particular road. Dumb luck . . .

# China House Commune Shootout, Late fall, 1967

I was hoping the phone wasn't for me . . . I wanted to give my late dinner a chance to digest a little before I hit the roads again. I knew I'd be out late, there'd been too much going on lately to expect to get much sleep before 3 AM.

"Weldon, sorry to bother you again, but you gotta get going. Some crazy gal said she'd just shinnied down a tree to get away from a shoot-out at the China House Commune. Do you know what she's talking about?"

What a dumb question! How the hell would I know? Oh, that's right, I know **everything** that's happening on my beat. The kids think I'm **"The Sheriff,"** never mind that I wasn't elected.

Crap! Sounds like an ambush setup. Dark, moonless night, a long, one-lane, dead-end dirt and gravel road, no easy turnaround, high embankment on one side, creek on the other, snipers shooting at patrol cars in Marin City and once at me on White's Hill. My partner was on his days off but I had him called anyway. Thank God he was home—most other Deputies wouldn't be able to find the place. It was the last house just above The Inkwell, a local swimming hole on Papermill Creek where it flows into Sam Taylor State Park. I put on my boots and jumped in the green-and-white, stuck my foot in the carburetor, then confirmed that Russ was on his way. No siren, just the bubblegum whirligig on top. Should I have the Fire Department stand by for injuries? Naw, let's check it out first, probably just a prank or a ruse to get me someplace else. Yeah, right . . . I made it from Nicasio to Lagunitas in under five minutes, tires and engine screaming their complaints.

I *did* know that the place was run by a tall, ruggedly handsome ex-Green Beret guy (looked like a giant Anglo Che Guevara and sometimes he still wore his beret). There were five or six women, a couple other guys, three or four young kids, one at the breast. They had a garden down near the creek and drank raw goat milk from three nannies that had the run of the place.

A flock of geese acted as unpaid security guards and usually intimidated any strangers, charging and hissing with their heads held low and outstretched. They got used to me eventually, thank God. The folks bought whole grains, barley, wheat and rolled oats in 20-pound sacks from the co-op down in Forest Knolls, another of the four communities in The Valley.

The house is two stories tall with a converted basement for more sleeping rooms. There was a "great room" divided by a waist-high bookshelf and a huge aquarium. There are redwood trees nearby. There was a rumor that **they smoked pot (!)** but they hadn't been any trouble, yet. I'd been there different times before, when the Louie family wanted to report a burglary or other problems, like nude sunbathers at the Inkwell. More recently, after the "hippie family" had moved in, I'd tried to locate someone with overdue traffic warrants. No problem, just get over to the Court House and square them away so I don't have to come back again and take you to Jail. The odor of grass wasn't significant enough for me to make a fuss.

I tried to slow the heady flow of adrenaline, anticipating Russ's reassuring voice to crackle over the air that he was "10-8, en route." As I turned off Sir Francis Drake Blvd., just west of Dead Man's Curve, I cut all my lights but found I needed the parking lights just to stay on the narrow road.

I'd had the guys down at the County garage modify all my light switches (interior dome, back-ups, brakes) so I could run dark. Sometimes I'd tuck my dual antennas into the rear windows so they wouldn't bang against low-hanging tree limbs. I felt more comfortable with a stacked deck . . . that's why I carried an H&R .22 Magnum derringer tucked behind my Sam Brown belt, and in the trunk kept a Model 94 Winchester .30-30, extra ammo for all my firearms, a chain saw, single-bit axe, old K-rations for those times I couldn't take a meal break, military first aid supplies (Kotex pads are good for the really big wounds), day-and-night aircraft flares for helicopter landings, 150 feet of climbing line, a pair of old leg irons from San Quentin Prison for the really violent ones or the ones who couldn't fit into a pair of handcuffs. Heavy-duty shocks and extra leafs in the rear springs helped, too.

I stopped below a low rise, short of the house, got out quietly, not latching the door, and listened while my eyes adjusted. All was quiet—good. I walked silently down the road, toes first, not letting my heels touch, not using my flashlight, damning my heart for beating so loudly. I was a Seneca Indian, one with the darkness, stealthily sneaking up on an enemy encampment, all of my senses vibrantly tuned. I tripped over a rock. Shit! I'm just glad I didn't drop my Remington 870 pump shotgun, loaded with four rounds of double-ought buckshot, the last round a one-ounce rifled slug for cars.

I never saw the towel draped over the rear license plate of the red and white Volkswagen Westphalia parked along the road. The bad guys were still around me and I didn't know it! This was eerie but good. If there had been a shooting, there should be loud voices, people running about, lots of lights in the other cottages and cabins. Nothing! Where's Russ?

I knocked lightly on the front door, the one at road level with the ornate Chinese carvings. No response, and it was locked. Damn! No chance of creeping inside. I went down the west side of the house and rapped on that door. Guevara came to the door, an Army Colt .45 pistol in his hand. I looked beyond him, wondering where the bad guys were, if there were any baddies at all, or if this was just another bad acid trip or somebody freakin' out on speed. The place was a mess. The tropical fish were still flopping on the floor after their tank had disintegrated in gunfire. Women were holding kids. **Everyone** was surprisingly calm. What's going on?

Guevara told me that three Marin City Blacks had come to that same door, one with a shotgun and the other two with handguns. They'd been there before, trying to buy some grass.

11

Guevara had stepped out of his bedroom at the opposite end of the great room with his .45 in hand and calmly ordered them, "Leave and nobody gets hurt, nobody has to know!"

"We want your grass, Man. We know you've got a bunch and we're gonna have it or you're gonna die!"

"Like Hell!"

The piano got it first. It was just inside the front door and Guevara had already killed more than enough people in 'Nam so he pulled his first shot to the right. That set of ivories won't ever sound the same. Everyone else in the house hit the deck between the front door and Guevara's bedroom door. Then Shotgun Man cut loose. First it was the fish tank, dumping maybe 80 fish and 250 gallons of water all over. Another round of birdshot bracketed Guevara's doorway, both sides and the ceiling. He picked up one small pellet in his thumb and another in his elbow, both on his shooting side, as he stood behind the jamb and returned fire. He was back in Pleiku except, dammit, he wouldn't kill again. All three rip-off artists were easy targets in the doorway maybe 20 yards away. Three shotgun blasts, four or five from the .45 yet, apparently, no one else was hit. Weird. Then they split . . . **really** weird.

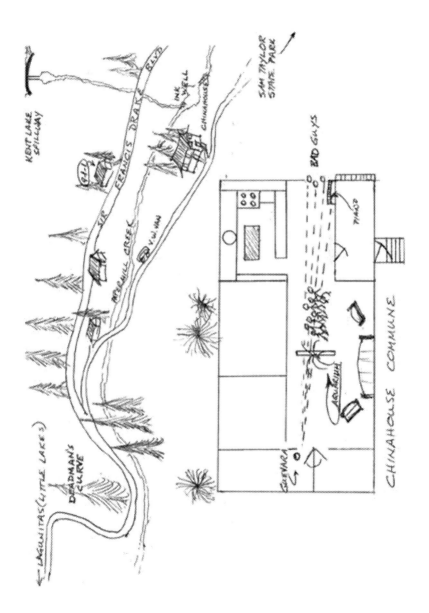

Dumb crooks—if they're going to go out prepared to shoot people they should use something bigger than #6 shot.

Lacy was naked, in a bedroom by herself, when the commotion started. I'd fantasized about her 20 year old lithe body when I saw her the first time a few weeks before. She knew about the dope and the frequent drug rip-offs around the County and the increasing levels of violence and lack of compassion. She wasn't dumb, she didn't lack courage and she wasn't wasting any time to get dressed. Maybe it was sheer terror. She slipped out of her second-floor window, wrapped her arms and legs around a huge redwood trunk and slithered down to the ground. Her cheeks, arms, vaginal lips, thighs, ankles and soles of her feet were bristling with redwood slivers. They can be real nasty and cause lingering infection. She stumbled down the embankment and across the smooth boulders in the creek, banging up her knees and ankles, then up the other side, across Sir Francis Drake, and rattled a neighbor's door. **That's** how I got the call.

Russ showed up, asked if I saw the VW van with the covered license plate. No . . . We excused ourselves, telling everyone to remain inside and quiet, then cautiously backtracked up the road. The van was gone! At least the immediate danger had evaporated. We put out a Code 777, the County-wide roadblock plan. We never did locate it and several years later learned that they had taken the long way home, gone farther West, down the Coast Highway and over Mt. Tamalpais back to Marin City. We didn't have people in the right places . . . guess they weren't as dumb as I thought.

I spent the next several hours and most of the next day dusting for prints, taking photographs, collecting spent cartridges, getting written statements, laboriously drawing out the crime scene.

It was a waste of time . . .

14

The "Inkwell" below Shafter Bridge
Sir Francis Drake Blvd., Lagunitas, California
Early 1900s

# Humor ~ Antidote for Exhaustion

Russ and I were pretty well pooped out from several long, hot and sticky summer days and nights of "keeping the peace" in the Valley, but we knew there wasn't much sense in turning in before the bars closed and the drunks either got home safely or had to be scraped up, sent to the hospital or booked. Rancho Nicasio was quiet, with only a few locals hanging out at the bar when we dropped in for a cup of java. It was good to get out of the patrol cars and stretch our legs. Dottie and Glenn were quietly going about their business of keeping the road house on course for the evening. I was sort of hoping that maybe Dottie would offer us some jumbo shrimp but that wasn't the case tonight.

Soon, Russ was slinking down on to the polished oak bar top and then he was sound asleep, his arms cradling his broken-nosed head. I very cautiously slipped his K-38 Smith and Wesson from its holster and placed it on the bar. The bartender, Joe Dentoni, who later became one of my Deputies after I made Sergeant, got a bottle of Wild Turkey and a couple of shot glasses for props. We spilled some water on the bar and tipped over one of the glasses.

Here we had a stinking-assed, dead drunk Deputy Sheriff passed out in the local watering hole. A fine example representing the mighty fine Marin County Sheriff's Department! I snapped a couple of shots from my 35 mm camera, very carefully put Russ's revolver back in its holster and eventually woke him up to get back on the road.

Russ was just a tad upset when I couldn't keep our not-so-little secret. I caved in and gave him the prints and negatives. I'm guessing he destroyed it all. All these years later . . . and I'm still wishing I had just one print.

16

# Rendering unto God

Halloween, 1967, darkness already set in, lots of kids in costume out and about in the San Geronimo Valley. No streetlights, no sidewalks, a few adults with the littler ones. I was one of those kids, except tonight I was a Mexican bandito in a Lone Ranger mask, a formal, rice hull sombrero and a serape draped over my shoulder. My mount wasn't "Silver" (as in "Hi-yo") but a green and white '64 Plymouth patrol car with gold seven-pointed stars embracing the Golden Gate Bridge on the doors. Another common factor was that in the trunk was my trusty Winchester Model '94 .30-30 lever-action carbine.

I also toted back there other supplies for 'most any eventuality: a single-bit axe for smashing in doors or clearing brush, a Homelight chain saw for downed trees (and firewood) which sometimes blocked critical roadways; battle dressings for major wounds; C-rations for two days; aerial maps of West Marin for search and rescue coordination; 150 feet of climbing line and carabiners for rappelling down steep cliffs; 'D' cell flashlight batteries; extra "double-ought" buckshot and rifled slugs for my Remington 870 12-guage pump shotgun, a box of .30-30s, and .357 Magnums, even ones for my .25 Beretta flip-top pistol and my Harrington & Richardson .22 Magnum double-barreled derringer which I sometimes carried tucked behind my Sam Brown belt. When I surreptitiously and casually hooked my gun hand over its butt, I could draw and fire two rounds faster than could be seen. I had a 30-power spotting scope for surveillance work; dairy boots for heavy mud or rain conditions; a length of lightweight chain with a pair of matched locks for really violent arrestees. No wonder the car sat low on its haunches—glad I had heavy-duty shocks.

None of that stuff helped me this night. Ever feel totally helpless in a violent situation? Like a deer blinded in the headlights or a field mouse scurrying from a swooping raptor?

17

Kirby C. S. D. was a crazed dope fiend. I learned later that he had swung a 240 pound woman by her long brown hair in several circles around his body and that, on another occasion, he had shoved the face of a local acidhead into a bonfire. I never knew why, except he was always crazy with angel dust and speed. I didn't meet him 'til Halloween. Wish I never had.

He came screaming past the Forest Knolls Lodge, over the Papermill Creek bridge in his beat-up old sedan and on up Montezuma Avenue. I tore off my mask, sombrero and serape and tossed 'em in the rear seat (in those days, we had no dividing screens), hit the lights and siren then stomped on the gas. Who was this idiot scattering kids into the darkness? Had to get him stopped before he killed someone. He pulled to a stop on the incline, jumped out and ran back to my patrol car. He'd left it in neutral and hadn't set the brake. It rolled backwards and slammed into my front bumper. I jumped out to meet him (didn't want him to get to me while I was still inside). He was about my size but looked a whole lot bigger. His arm shot out quicker than I could react, his hand grabbing me by the neck and lifting me up on my toes at arm's length. At the time, I was a tad under six feet and weighed 197 pounds, without my gear.

"God damn you, Travis, I'm going to render you unto God!"

How did he know me? Had I ever arrested him or otherwise hassled him? Who in Hell is this guy? I was in big trouble. I hadn't had time to call in the stop and I knew that my partner was in Fairfax, maybe five miles away. His hand was a vise, clamping and restricting the blood flowing in my carotid arteries and the air in my windpipe. Little green explosions were popping in front of my eyes and I was starting to lose consciousness. "Put me down," I rasped. "Do you believe in God?", he demanded. "Yes, put me down." I was going to have to shoot him before I passed out. I knew I couldn't overcome him physically and I didn't want to die that night. He dropped me and turned away, towards his commune, as it turned out. "You're under arrest for assault and battery on a peace officer!" DID I SAY THAT? You fool! No help around that I knew of. I felt like slapping my mouth shut but the words were already out instinctively (horses out of the barn now, why shut to doors?). Oops, now what do I do?

Kirby saved me unknown grief for the time being. "I'm not going anywhere with you until I get some cigarettes." He walked away a few houses up the hill and I got on the radio and called in a "940A" (as in "I need help RIGHT NOW"!). Lots of the other guys on the road that night didn't know much about the Valley, couldn't find their way around. My partner, Russ, at least knew the location. Thank God for little favors.

Kirby came back from his house with a fresh pack of Marlboros and got in the front passenger seat while I was behind the wheel. Why had I left that unlocked? Beats me. Some of his housemates followed him down as Russ arrived there in just a few minutes. He could drive hard and knew where he was going. Kirby seemed to have settled down and was ready to go to Jail. Small problem, though: he needed to be handcuffed and put in the rear seat.

Russ had his riot helmet on as he came up to my window. I briefed him while Kirby glared at him. Russ leaned in and asked Kirby, "How ya doing?" That's all it took. Kirby let out a low growl and lunged across my lap to grab Russ's helmet, pulling it off and tearing Russ's ear, trying to grab his Smith & Wesson K-38 out of its holster. I got it first and shoved it down between the seat and the door. Russ had Kirby's head in my crotch and was grappling with his flailing arms. I was really worried that he would bite my family jewels or, worse yet, get one of our revolvers. I got mine out and shoved it under my thigh. The red light was still on and, when the horn ring is depressed, it activates the siren.

His buddies streamed out of their commune as piranhas to meat and swarmed around the passenger side, trying to pull Kirby out the door. I managed to get Kirby's left arm in a hammerlock. This was getting crazy and just about out of control. Russ got free, unlimbered his riot baton, and went around to the passenger side, swinging as he went. The opportunistic bastards fell back and just watched. Russ and I got to the business of hooking Kirby up and moving him to the back seat. He'd settled down again. The road was too narrow to turn around and all the folks compounded the challenge of getting out of there in one piece.

I knew that the narrow fire trail at the top of the canyon, a back way to get us into San Geronimo and back on to Sir Francis Drake Blvd., was passable. I took off with Russ protecting my rear from any who might pursue us. The trip to the crisis unit was uneventful and my heart beat returned to normal. Adrenaline rushes become pleasantly addictive but I'd had enough for one night—you might say I overdosed.

Eventually, Kirby plead guilty to misdemeanor assault on a police officer, did a few days in Jail and made restitution for my shredded shirt and other minor stuff. Russ's ear healed.

Several weeks later, with my partner on his days off, Kirby was acting up again. He had moved farther up the canyon after he got out of Jail. I'm guessing his roommates figured he was too crazy even for them. Now the redwoods were telling him to kill his older neighbor lady with a double-bitted axe. Damn . . . I don't want to do this again. Funny thing about paranoid schizophrenics: one can never tell what they're going to do or what's going through their heads. After interviewing the lady, I met Kirby and his axe in his front yard. He SEEMED to be calm. "Trepidation" had a new meaning for me and, yet, I was strangely calm, too. I listened to him for a while, ready to draw and fire if I had to. He confirmed, not unsurprisingly, what the lady had said. I took what I hoped was an imperceptible deep breath and told Kirby that he was thinking bad thoughts and needed to go to the crisis unit. He squinted at me, gazed

20

up to the towering trees as if seeking advice, then shifted back to me for what seemed an eternity. "Okay, let's go!" Whew . . . dodged THAT bullet!

Thank you, God, again . . .

# George Gallagher ~ Pig Rancher & Deer Hunter

George comes from an early-day Nicasio ranching family. He's smallish, with a big heart, a falsetto voice and a sensitivity for the land. He and his brothers had a hog and cattle ranching business down at the T-intersection by Nicasio Reservoir. Sometimes the hogs would wander across the Petaluma-Pt. Reyes Road to wallow in the shoreline mud of the reservoir. More than once on dark nights, a motorist would ram into one of his huge pigs and mess up both car and porker.

I had a civil paper to serve on George, nothing serious, and went to his house down the road a ways. His wife told me he and a bunch of his friends were deer hunting a few miles away in the canyons along Wilson Hill. George was getting along in years so he was sitting down near the base of a canyon as some of the younger guys were hopefully driving the deer toward the older ones.

I drove through a Portagee gate (a couple of posts suspending three or four strands of barbed wire) then hiked toward some pickup trucks. I spotted George's International jeep and figured I'd find him, hopefully without messing up the hunt. I stayed in the open and moved slowly—didn't want to get shot by accident. Pretty soon I heard a big one come crashing down through the oaks and madrones, then the nearby sharp crack of a rifle. I moved that way and found George sprawled on the hillside between some big rocks. That big ol' buck had come leaping and bounding right into the muzzle of George's rifle just as he stood up, busted his shoulder and knocked him ass over teakettle downhill.

George looked up at me with a kind of dazed expression on his face and, in that high voice of his asked, "Weldon, how did you get here so quick?" I just grinned at him. The "legend" just seemed to grow all by itself. I rigged up a sling for his shoulder and gave him his paper. I think the hunt continued after a few laughs and George took care of himself. Can't remember exactly.

# Oak Tree Inn ~ two of 'em

My partner and I heard a dispatch to Southern Marin deputies to check out a disturbance call at the Oak Tree Inn, down on the Sausalito waterfront. There had been several violent brawls there, mostly brought on by the Blacks of Marin City flexing their muscles after the 60's Civil Rights movement. I had been part of that early on.

We swung into the Rancho Nicasio for some java around 10:00 PM and palavered with the locals for a bit, then returned to our patrol cars.

Dispatch asked the Southern deputies if they had handled the call. Everything had been quiet down there. Russ and I were energized when Dispatch advised that two guys had been fighting with cue sticks ever since the first call and that the owner, Ray B., was wondering where in Hell the deputies were.

That's OUR Oak Tree Inn! Ray had bought it from Dean and trouble had been brewing for a few weeks in San Geronimo.

I screwed on my riot helmet, snugged down my lap belt and tore out from the Rancho for the six-mile run.

Ray was a scrawny little guy, maybe 5 foot, four. He was behind in his agreed-upon payments to Dean, so Dean decided to remove some old Western prints and stuffed game heads from the walls in compensation. I didn't know that Dean was the other combatant.

Entering the joint on the run, I unsnapped my holster and charged in with my baton at the ready. They were streaming blood and still trading punches. What the Hell? The little guy, being the owner, just had to be right.

I leaped into the fray and came down hard with my baton on the big guy's head (not approved policy). A bystander (cousin to Dean) said, "Hey, that's not right!'

My .357 Magnum dropped on the floor in their midst. I straddled it with my baton at port arms as Dean swung around, wiping blood out of his eyes and recognizing. me. "Travis, you little shit, I thought I told you how to hit harder than that!" Whew!

Ray placed Dean under "citizen's arrest," but Dean said that he wasn't going anywhere until he'd had a beer. Ray refused, so Dean poured himself a draft.

Off we went to Marin General Hospital for several stitches, then to Jail. I took a Polaroid photo and woke up Dean's wife to explain why he would not be available to complete his milk delivery that morning.

# Disturbing the "Piece"

Marin County has two halves: the Highway 101 corridor, where most of the businesses and virtually *all* of the Cities and incorporated Towns are situated. Then there is WEST Marin, another environment altogether, with dairy ranches, mini-horse estates, hippie communes; villages whose occupants or ancestors came from Oklahoma and Arkansas to build *Victory,* then *Liberty Ships* down in Sausalito during World War II, or the survivors of the Great Fire (and Earthquake) in San Francisco in 1906.

Highway 101 is the main North-and-South arterial highway that runs the length of California, border to border. Sir Francis Drake Blvd. runs East and West, bisecting the County laterally. Out on the Coast, the venerable Highway One gingerly and cautiously snakes above the Pacific Ocean, skirting precipitous and deadly cliffs (oh, how well I know . . .)

Late one summer evening I'd finally had to take a minor offender into San Rafael for booking at the Jail for a batch of unpaid traffic warrants after repeated requests and warnings. After socializing with the Desk Sergeant, I picked up the interoffice mail for our Pt. Reyes Substation and was coming back over White's Hill onto my home turf. No more street lights, sidewalks, convenience stores or hustle-bustle. A dark peacefulness descended over me as I headed West toward the Coast, but with the headlights providing good visibility on the moonless night. Stay Alert! This long day is almost over. Must keep a sharp eye out for deer and fox, but mostly for any loose cattle. I was longing to park the patrol car at home and crawl into bed with my patient, understanding wife, Mary Lou, without disturbing her slumber. Thank God, she understood and accepted my passion and devotion to "duty," even though it came after our marriage. She was a good wife.

Up ahead, the taillights of a slow moving vehicle loomed. Probably a drunk, I guessed. I thought, "Damn! I sure as hell don't want to add another two or three hours on to my already long day, what with an arrest, vehicle impoundment and writing a report available for the Sergeant's review and on to the District Attorney by 9:00 AM the next day."

I had a duty, though, I told myself. I couldn't let him drive into another occasional oncoming car and kill a bunch of folks. Besides, my Resident Sergeant, Bob Bertrand, would see how really dedicated and professional I was.

I could see he was the only occupant, so knew that I wouldn't have more than one guy to deal with. No need to request a back-up. I fell in closer behind him for a while, observing and noting for my Arrest Report how his speed varied as he wandered back and forth, mostly within the single lane but occasionally drifting onto the shoulder or into the oncoming lane, then lurching back again. This guy is either really sleepy or highly intoxicated. The driver obviously was oblivious to me being behind him.

I hit both the red light and "bubble-gum machine" switches and tapped the horn ring for the siren. Up popped a blond, long-haired woman, sitting bolt-upright in the front passenger seat! A quick, quirky thought passed through my mind: that's not the only thing in that car that's bolt upright!

They pulled over right away. I checked the driver's I.D., ran a warrant check and I made sure that everything was copasetic with the two of them.

I sped off, leaving them to recompose themselves at roadside.

"Disturbing the Peace" (PC § 415) in the California Penal Code means loud, boisterous behavior, challenging to fight and so on.

This night, I was guilty of "Disturbing a Piece" in quite another way.

Mary Lou didn't get much sleep that night.

# Suicide in Progress

I was heading back from the new Civic Center when dispatch told me to respond to a "suicide in progress" on twisty Lucas Valley Road, which runs from the Highway 101 corridor back out to my stomping grounds (and patrol responsibilities) in West Marin.

A weird thought coursed through my mind as I stomped on the accelerator: either someone is thinking about it or it's already a done deal. Well, it was "in progress," alright, and weird it was.

The victim's wife responded to my door knock. She said, "He's back there," pointing to the two-bedroom area of the cottage and told me that he was despondent over a pending surgery, then she went back to washing dishes. A shot rang out. More weirdness.

He had been diagnosed with a terminal cancerous growth beneath a clavicle and was scheduled for surgery that morning. He instead had decided to carve it out himself with a paring knife. Their bed was blood-saturated, the hall across to the opposite bedroom was a crimson trail. He had managed to retrieve a .22 rifle from the closet and shoot himself into his mouth and brain.

I think he was dead, but if he wasn't, I was going to let him die anyway; his choice, not mine.

His wife, a non-resident from England, remained eerily calm as we awaited the Coroner. She had no friends in this country, nor did they have any significant or supportive relationships within the tiny rural community of Nicasio. She had no one to turn to. It is hard to imagine what sort of relationship the two of them had.

I was stymied. What can I do to sort this all out and do something that is right, good, proper and helpful?

I gathered up the blood-soaked quilts, blankets, sheets and pillows and threw them in the trunk of the patrol car. The new widow and I got some Clorox from under the sink and got down on our hands and knees together and scrubbed and scrubbed.

I left her, alone, to make arrangements to fly back home to England. What a bummer.

At home, I washed all of that stuff three times but it was useless. It all went to the dump.

My emotions and some of my sanity took a dump, too.

# Burglary Buggery

5:40 AM on a weekday morning and I was hoping to get some more shut-eye but duty rang me up. Someone was stuck in the chimney at the San Geronimo Golf Course Club House. The usual jolt of adrenalin subsided as I got dressed—the guy wasn't going anywhere soon. The Head Groundskeeper had been getting the golf carts out of the underground garage when he heard some hollering coming from the dining room area. He didn't know what to think of it, but a cautious investigation led him to a pair of dangling feet inside the fireplace.

Russ was off-duty that day, so I asked for a back-up from the Main Office. Deputy Dave was my man. He was, and still is, a Mormon Bishop (Church of Latter Day Saints) with a dry sense of humor. We arrived about the same time, evaluated what we had, and hatched a plan. We clambered onto the roof and hollered down the chimney, "Hey Mister—what are you doing down there?" "I'm stuck, damn it, get me out of here!" "Hey Dave, did you bring some rope like I asked?" "What rope, nobody said anything about rope." "Well, now what are we gonna do—do you want to go all the way back to San Rafael or should we wake up the Fire Department?" "C'mon Guys, get me out of here!" That chimney has some great acoustics so I started reciting the Miranda Rights to him in a slow, deep and resonant tone, hoping that he was thinking that maybe God was devilishly reprimanding him for his transgressions. He didn't appreciate it much. We hauled him up with my climbing line, hooked him up and started our minimal investigation.

It seems that he had just gotten out of San Quentin Prison and needed more walking around money than the few dollars he'd been given. His girlfriend dropped him off around midnight with a hank of clothesline, then left. He'd tied one end to a vent shaft and lowered himself down, not realizing that most chimney flues have a zigzag above the fire pit. That chimney had an unglazed terra cotta lining, with a sharp edge

30

on top. When "Bungling Burglar" tried to haul himself back up, the rope parted and down he went, really buggered up.

He languished in Jail for fourteen days and during one of his preliminary hearings, Judge Alvin, noted for his liberalism, released him with "Time Served," justifying it, I was told, by the fact that "he had been out of prison an insufficient time to readjust to a law-abiding environment." Huh?? If I recall correctly, even San Quentin didn't want to violate his presumed parole. It was a head-scratcher.

That same judge testified for me later on, after I was fired (see back pages).

Another early morning call to the same club house was very much different. It was an early morning "smash-and-grab" burglary of the pro shop, with a large, plate glass door being broken out and armloads of clothing flung into a getaway car. The alarm went off and, by the time I got the call, a Main Office Deputy ("Buzz") had pursued three black guys over a narrow cart bridge above Nicasio Valley Road to the "back nine" holes. They bailed out behind the Lagunitas School as Buzz dented their rear bumper with a .38 round.

That same Head Groundskeeper joined me trying to track the bad guys. He was an experienced hunter and I had had some training by a notable professional tracker, having been taught by a Native American. Most folks are unaware that the smell of sweat (and other bodily fluids) varies not only with diet but also with stress. When fear, anxiety, anger or illness is present, there is a noticeable difference in the scent—much more pungent and offensive. That morning, the heavy fog was still lingering and held the scent close to the ground. Between the two of us we tracked someone a mile or so where the sign petered out along Sir Francis Drake Blvd.

We had extra deputies patrolling about for some time while I went back to the scene and laboriously dusted the many shards of glass for latent fingerprints. Many of the community members were aware of the event and there were very few black residents living there. As I worked toward the last of the pile of

31

glass, BINGO! I lifted three and a half perfect prints from one shard. I guessed correctly that it had been stuck in the frame and had been removed for safety by one of the crooks.

Inspector Ken Irving, my mentor with a fabulous memory, recalled that there had been a "till tap" theft from a gas station in Fairfax a few months earlier by three black guys involving a yellow Chevy "Corvair" with "272" in the license plate. As he was working that end, he received a call from an East Bay police Department about a couple of guys peddling golf clothing. Two down, one to go. Around 10:00 AM, a local resident spotted the third suspect hitchhiking along Sir Francis Drake Blvd. I screamed down there to hook him up. He was disheveled, to say the least, with dried grasses stuck in his hair and clothing. I recognized his stench.

Many of us pulled it all together and three crooks went to prison.

# Abbott's Lagoon Drifter
### and
# Russ's Rubber Face

We'd had some violence in West Marin recently, most brought on by acid or the dope trade—the relative remoteness and proximity to San Francisco and the East Bay made it a convenient area to dump bodies from other jurisdictions. Some died of relatively natural causes, such as an accidental drug overdose, some were murdered over dope deals gone bad, rip-offs, paybacks, territorial disputes. Two of our informants were forcibly injected with fatally pure heroin (to make it look like an accident); one had his head crushed with a crowbar; others were shot at close range. Their bodies were incinerated in their cars or stuffed in the trunk and/or pushed over an oceanside cliff or wrapped in a bloody rug and left alongside the roadway. One young man left a note with his carefully folded clothing on a cliff out by Chimney Rock. He'd taken some great L.S.D. and now knew for certain that he could fly. He'd see all of his friends in the Wild Blue Yonder. His body and his parents were crushed. Later, we had a series of "Trailside Killings" linked to David Carpenter who ultimately was convicted of several, both in Marin and in Santa Cruz County down on the peninsula.

More recently, two young lady-friends were having a quiet, reacquainting picnic out at Abbott's Lagoon. Francine had lived in Inverness Park for a while but Becca had moved to Iowa a couple of years before. To get to the Lagoon, you have to go out Sir Francis Drake through Inverness, bear right on Pierce Point Road after you go over twisty Doc Ottinger's Hill, then look for a small parking area on the left. Leave your car there and hike maybe a mile down toward 10-Mile Beach (some call it North Beach), across gently rolling terrain populated with sedges and low grasses and, in the springtime, a beautiful scattering of miniature wildflowers and shrubs—yellow bush lupine and bright orange monkeyflower with their clown-face blossoms. Monet would be enthralled and wished that he'd had his paint box.

In the wintertime about ten days after a typhoon in Japan, we used to comb the beach for hand-blown-glass fishing-net floats, some as big as soccer balls wrapped in hand-tied twine, most more like tennis balls, that drifted across the Pacific. Once, when out with a local rancher, George Nunes, my share filled my old Navy sea bag to the top. I gave most away as presents over the years.

Nighttime in the general area, you might see some axis or spotted fallow deer, imported decades ago from Europe and maintaining a fairly constant herd size. They used to be a good source of legal meat for the locals, until Fish & Game had them declared official game animals. Now, they're a good source of illegal meat for the locals. There's ground squirrels, 'possums, badgers, wildcats, coyotes, cougars, a flourishing herd of re-introduced Tule elk, Barn owls with their white, heart-shaped faces, Great Horned owls, Red-tailed hawks, Peregrine falcons, Great Blue herons, white and brown pelicans, meadowlarks, flickers, barn swallows and shore birds and on and on . . .

Fortunately, at least during the week, there are not many people, maybe one or two parked cars. It's peaceful and quiet, a place to let yourself drift in one of God's back yards.

The drifter slowed up in his battered old Plymouth stationwagon as the women were walking away from their car. He drove off a little, waited several minutes, made a U-turn, came back and parked next to their car. Now they were getting smaller and smaller, their lower bodies gradually fading from his view as they slowly walked down toward the swale, toting a basket of gourmet delicacies and a natural-dyed Angora goat wool blanket, woven by The Black Mountain Weaver in Pt. Reyes Station. They had a lot of catching up to do and they meant to have this magical place be the location for a memorable chapter in their long-lasting and sweet friendship. They loved and respected each other in that special, affectionate way that

34

men can't (or won't) try to fathom, yet they had chosen, so far, to not engage in sexual experimentation.

The drifter reached under the piles of clothing and other stuff in the back seat and pulled out the WW II-vintage M-1 .30 caliber carbine with the 15-round clip already inserted. He'd last used it up in Medford in a Mom-and-Pop Stop'n'Rob, but he hadn't needed to shoot anyone then. So far, so good, but damn, he was so horny he had blue balls that hurt when he walked. These two gals looked ripe for plucking. Pretty, maybe 25 and 28, good figures, out-of-state plates on their car so they might not come back to testify if he got careless.

He sat there behind the wheel, his right hand caressing the cool wooden stock of the carbine, his middle finger going in and out of the trigger guard as he messaged his cock and testicles. He got a raging hard-on, his vision blurred a little as he squinted for a last glimpse before the bitches moved out of sight, making sure of their final direction. The younger one, the one with the long, flowing blond hair reminded him of his step-sister, the one his Dad had forcibly deflowered when he thought she was ready for it at fifteen. She hated him after that, and who could blame her? Drifter and his Dad never hunted together after that.

Drifter slipped out of the car and threw a windbreaker jacket over the carbine before he began the stalk. He wasn't in any hurry—they were easy prey. He was between them and their car; the sun was somewhat behind him but still rising; a steady, mild sea breeze wafting inland muffled his footsteps through the grasses and dissipated any of his musk. Mother Nature was helping him three ways.

Funny how hunting for animals to eat or mount on a wall can turn into stalking humans to—, to do—, what? "Mount" them—that's a good one! What **will** I do with them? Maybe they'll like me. Maybe all three of us could have a really good time out here in the open with the sun warming our naked and entangled bodies! Maybe they've got some cold wine. Doesn't matter, I'm on my way—we'll just see how it plays out. God! I'm on a real high and it's not those two Buds I had for breakfast, either. Gotta remember to be careful in case it gets nasty.

A quarter mile down, he spotted them again, maybe 50 yards this side of the lagoon. They had laid out the blanket and had just poured some Sebastiani chenin blanc into ecologically-correct paper cups, thinking of a toast to their warm relationship. Francine, the blond one, saw him over Rebecca's shoulder. She was surprised and just a little nervous to see another person nearby. She said to Becca in a calm, quiet voice that a guy was approaching them but not to get excited about it. Becca twisted around to take a look and had a sense of immediate discomfort. Maybe it was his irregular gait as he drew closer, or his gaze fixed upon them, or seeing that he hadn't shaved for a few days. And what was he carrying wrapped in the jacket? It obviously wasn't a walkingstick, otherwise he'd have it out.

Now Francie squirmed a little, then stood up to face him. This was not good. They were a long way from any help, even out of earshot to anyone. "Stay calm," said told herself. **"Think!** Don't telegraph any fear. If you think there's no way to avoid physical confrontation, if you have to kick, scratch, bite, scream, run—take swift action **first**."

Her sifu's voice, the one who taught her a street survival course when she was going to UCLA, came through to her in his strangely familiar, calm, almost soothing, sing-song voice. Thank you Master Chen! Francie took a couple of steps to get closer, screwed on her best smile, placed her hands on her hips and jutted out her breasts. It was her best impersonation of Wonder Woman she could muster. It probably looked pretty comical, she mused, even as her heart pounded and the morning unfolded.

As soon as Becca stood up, the carbine came out. "All right ladies, how's it gonna be? We gonna have some fun or do I get rough?"

Becca recoiled in fright and horror at their sudden predicament, stumbling backward and tripping over a clump of monkeyflower. Drifter instinctively swung toward her as she fell away to his left. He racked in a round with his left thumb under the receiver as his right hand squeezed the pistol grip tightly. Francie sprang in from his right, grabbed the forestock and kicked his groin with her right foot so hard that it lifted him completely off the ground and hurt her instep. The carbine was in **her** hands now as Drifter rolled around in a tight fetal position, hands and arms down low between his thighs, howling and moaning with the sickening, overwhelming pain. She must have literally ruptured his balls, they were so engorged. He sounded like a dog that had just been run over by a car. Francie pounced on him like a wolverine, swinging down with the carbine and kicking for all she was worth. The stock broke at the pistol grip and still she beat, beat, beat. Now Becca, getting her wits about her as her anger over being violated welled up within her, joined in the punishment, kicking him viciously in the ribs. Drifter was bleeding heavily around his face, head and neck. They may have broken one or both arms and certainly some ribs. No way were they going to walk away if he had the slightest chance of following.

They quickly scooped up their things, together with the three pieces of the carbine, and hustled back to the car. Drifter stayed behind, seeming to melt into the sandy, grassy soil. Hysterical, giddy, joyful laughter overcame them as they made their getaway. They nearly wrecked as they snaked down though the twisties of Ottinger's Hill, overwhelming relief flowing through them. They had survived! They could still enjoy their friendship! Life **can** turn out okay . . .

Francie knew where the substation was and that they were going to report it to The Sheriff. As they gradually calmed down, Becca reflected on a granite engraving they recently had seen at the Palace of the Legion of Honor overlooking the San Francisco Presidio. It was a quote by Frances E. Willard, an early suffragette, as she stood on that spot in 1883: "We are one world of tempted humanity." If only Frances could have seen them today! Her literary mind shifted to what Oscar

37

Wilde might have said about Drifter: "The only way to get rid of temptation is to yield to it." Bad advice today.

I was putting the finishing touches on a burglary report when these two good-looking women parked out front and came into the substation. Well! This will brighten up my day—probably tourists who lost their way. They were cute and perky, walking with a certain confidence, might say exuberance.

"We'd like to report a crime," said Francine matter-of-factly as I opened the screen door. I drew up some chairs and listened carefully and somewhat incredulously. Could they be concocting this tale, riding on the heels of the other stuff going on, hoping for a little bit of personal notoriety? They were too calm, no obvious injuries, had too clear of a recollection, too many details for having experienced what they were telling me. "Where's this gun you broke over the guy's head?" (Bet they didn't figure I'd ask them that!) "Oh, it's out in the car—I'll get it for you."

Sure enough, there it was—the shattered stock, receiver and barrel, forestock and clip missing. I pulled back the bolt and ejected the one live round. Wow! Some story. And we have a chance of catching this son-of-a-bitch, if he's still alive!

I had enough notes about Drifter's description and car and Francine's and Rebecca's personal information. Francine still lived in the Bay Area and Becca said she would be around for a few more days to identify the guy when we found him. What a pair! I got ahold of Sgt. Bertrand and filled him in. My partner, Russ, had showed up and Jerry Tanner, the fun-loving Resident Deputy who lived in Inverness Park, was on his days off and not home. Jerry later died in a family boating accident in Tomales Bay. We never did find his body, after looking for three days. Sharks or crabs ate him; maybe he drifted all the way out to the ocean with the tide.

Sgt. Bob came up with a great idea: We were in the midst of harvesting the marijuana crops just before the growers got to them. We had a cooperative effort going with C.A.M.P. (Campaign Against Marijuana Planting), a multi-County operation using Shasta County's helicopter to haul out the stacks of plants that had been cut down by squads of Deputies. Shasta is up North with Humboldt and Trinity Counties in the "Emerald Triangle" where the premium grass is grown as the primary cash crop, contributing in large measure to the local economy. We got approval to divert the chopper for an immediate search of the area. At the same time, Constable Mike McLean and his bloodhounds, Brandy and Little One, got to working. We set up a road block at Pierce Point Road and Sir Francis Drake Blvd. after determining that Drifter's car was still parked. We had him—there was only one way out, at least by road, and judging from what the gals had done to him, he wasn't walking very far.

The chopper criss-crossed the area for a couple hours in a checker-board pattern, refueled at Hamilton Field then returned until dusk. The hounds picked up the scent from clothing in the stationwagon, tracked down to the lagoon, North along the beach for a while, then lost it, apparently in the surf line. This guy was using some pretty good survival skills.

By nightfall, we still didn't have him. Rats—here was a wonderful chance to show how effective we were at protecting the community and, even with a jump-start, we weren't cutting it. We maintained the roadblock that night, hoping he wouldn't sneak by us in the darkness. We'd disabled his car and would check each one coming out past us. We figured he didn't still have a gun at least, or did he? A couple of times, I got out of my patrol car and squatted in the brush a few hundred yards up the road, thinking maybe I'd hear better, or maybe spot him in the scant moonlight—at the least I wouldn't be an easy target and I'd be able to get the jump on him. Each time I got to shivering so uncontrollably I had to get back in the car to raise my body temperature, hypothermia was a concern.

Jerry came home and relieved me along about one in the morning. I filled him in and joshed him about not keeping a clean beat. He took it pretty well—I knew he was hoping to catch the baddie himself that night.

Next morning, still no good news. Joe Dentoni took over on the roadblock and I had the opportunity of snooping around by myself. I searched every damn building from the roadblock to the McClure Ranch. Hot and sweaty, bits of hayseed in my hair and uniform, I took a break back at the substation. Fortunately, things were quiet on my own beat in the Valley and by now, every decent person on the Peninsula knew what had happened. Some brought out snacks and hot coffee—damned nice folks.

If I were Drifter, where would I be, how would I get out of this mess?

Drifter hadn't lost his senses and he knew we'd probably be looking for him to be heading South. One thing he'd learned from his Dad was patience. He headed North, although he had no idea the only thing that awaited him was the Pacific ocean on one side and the mouth of Tomales Bay on the other. He made it all the way out to the McClure Ranch, then realized he was trapped at the end of nowhere. He'd seen a pretty coffee-table book at Toby's Feed Barn in town—something about "An Island in Time" but hadn't picked it up to look at it, afraid of looking like a shoplifter. In his pained and dulled mind, he had a sort of epiphany, like maybe his own time was running out. He hid out in an implement shed 'til it was good and dark. The Mexican family that was employed there headed out, probably in to town or to visit down the road. Drifter saw his chance to get some food. God knows when he'd eat again.

The cottage was unlocked and he gathered up as much stuff as he thought would go unnoticed, mostly canned foods which he could open with his Swiss Army knife, a half-loaf of French bread and one bottle of Dos Equis beer. At least they had good taste in beer! And he'd have a bottle for water. Leaving scant tracks, he made for the large barn which was pretty much stuffed with baled hay. He rearranged some of the bales into a little igloo-type enclosure up high in the mow that would keep him warm with body heat and out of sight. Then he remembered the dogs. He went below again and gathered up

40

some dried pasture pancakes, took them above and broke them around his hideout to hide his scent.

After eating, then checking his caked wounds as best he could, he fell into a fitful half-sleep, knowing he would have to be alert to the slightest sign of approach. His aching ribs kept him from falling too deeply into the abyss. Before daylight, the cows ambled amicably toward the barn, with full udders swaying. Time to get moving. The soreness was really setting in. He knew he had some broken ribs and gashes on his face, hoped none of his innards were ruptured. Skirting the road, picking his way through the chaparral, he made maybe three miles before a rancher's wife spotted him. She could have taken him herself, beat up as he was, but called the S/O.

We hooked him up and took him to the substation for interrogation. After a cockamamie bullshit claim of running off the road and crashing his car, I took him "over the Hill" and booked him for ADW and attempt 261 PC (assault with a deadly weapon and attempted rape). He pled guilty and, in view of his extensive rap sheet from across the mid-West, went to prison for a long time. Good community effort!

* * *

Russ has a crooked, busted nose from a few fights when he was in the Air Force—one nostril doesn't let much air through it. Constable McLean had acquired a two-phase molding compound (moulage) that we could use to replicate tire, weapon and dead body facial impressions. One quiet after noon out at the substation we decided to experiment with it. We heated up and melted the two components in a sauce pan in the tiny kitchen (which also served as our armory for recovered weapons). Russ was clean shaven so a smooth impression could be molded. He lay down on Judge Dave Baty's beat-up old desk, with a couple of straws protruding from his nostrils and a Penal Code as a pillow. I started to paint his face with the warm glop, using a one-inch brush. A human skull gazed down from the window ledge behind the desk (McLean's macabre humor,

41

again). Russ, as usual, was resolute. I would have had a sense of suffocation and claustrophobia.

My devious, mischievous mind started to crank over as I waited patiently for the rubbery stuff to set. Later, we would pour plaster of Paris into it to make a hard positive image. I told Russ to just lay there and relax while I went into the S/O portion of the little building to log in some warrants. There were two telephone lines, one for the Court and one for us. I rang up one, then answered the other, watching Russ through the connecting door:

"Pt. Reyes Sheriff's substation, Deputy Travis, how may I help you"?

A long pause, then, "Where's this? "Yeah, I know where it is. Are you SURE he's dead? A rope around his neck? How many times was he shot?!?"

That was all it took. Russ bolted upright, pulling the straws out of his nostrils and tearing off the rubber face, grabbing for his Sam Brown gun belt. I watched him for a minute and he couldn't figure out why I wasn't already out the door. Big laugh at Russ's expense. Wish some of the other guys could have seen it.

That night, Russ had a call after he'd crawled into bed with his wife, Sherrie. He left his plaster head in a wig on his pillow for her to "find" in the morning when she awakened.

We're just a little bit weird . . .

# My partner, Russell Brown Hunt

# Date with My Sister

My youngest sister, Carla ("Kitty" to family) was a gentle soul, a pretty young woman who loved animals, especially horses, and would often bring home injured critters of all sorts, often, but not always, healing them. As an adult, she had a one-eyed screech owl that she had rescued and became a family member. He had a cage that Carla provided for him but he was free to come and go through an open window in an extra bedroom up in her Sonoma County country home, just North of Marin.

One day, when we were still living at the family home in Woodacre, she brought home an injured skunk and presented it to me. I named her Daisy. She was almost blind and had equilibrium difficulties, frequently tilting forward onto her nose, which caused her tail to suddenly uplift as if to spray her defensively pungent perfume. I thought about rabies but decided to keep her, foolishly, to wait and see. She survived just fine but, because of her canned dog food diet in captivity, became constipated and ill. The local vet in Fairfax suggested a male name so *she* became Daisy Joe. The Doc gave him a shot of Penicillin and an enema and all was fine for several months until he escaped and a dog took after him. The neighborhood skunk-stunk for days!

At fifteen, Kitty fell in love with a nice young man who had had a troubled youth and had been raised largely in Saint Anselm's School in nearby San Anselmo. George came to love horses, the red '49 Ford they bought and playing boogie-woogie on our piano.

They married early and he enlisted in the Marine Corps, serving a tour of duty in Viet Nam. She was also a gourmet cook, a good gardener, knew how to make herself look even more attractive and had a way of making a gracious, comfy home anywhere she lived.

Later on, without consulting with his wife, George reenlisted for more service, again in Viet Nam. Kitty moved back with our parents.

She missed him and worried about his safety a whole lot. He'd already killed nineteen Viet Cong or NVA regulars. On a whim to lift her spirits and provide some "safe" male companionship, I invited her out for a dinner and movie date one evening in March of 1968. As I was walking out my door, the phone rang and Sgt. Wade Powell gave me the bad news. George had been killed—at the siege of Khe Sahn during the Tet Offensive. I learned later that half of his head and most of one shoulder had been blown off by an RPG (Rocket Propelled Grenade). He had been waiting to board a waiting helicopter to start his homeward journey, when pressed into service to help carry a wounded warrior to the chopper, according to his corporal who was with him.

I also learned later that Kitty often had nightmares of two uniformed Marines appearing at the door. She would wake up screaming, waking our parents, and the Marines would go away once again.

This night, because of the unlit, meandering roads of Woodacre, the Marines had asked for escort guidance from the Sheriff's Department. Wade had the compassionate consideration and good sense to have me, instead of the on-duty Deputy, Russ Hunt, meet them at the Fire Department Headquarters in Woodacre. Good! Kitty was expecting me any way and, that way, it would allow me to be with her when she realized her nightmares had come true.

I lived close to Woodacre, beat it out to the firehouse and waited for the Marines. I waited, and waited some more. Where in Hell *were* they? I called Sgt. Powell who told me that the Marines had already completed their mission. Damn it! And *damn them!* Didn't they see the value of having me with them; or did they just not want another family member there?

My dear, sweet, little sister, Kitty, pretty and pregnant with her third child, had answered the door; all dressed up

45

and ready for her "date" with me but, instead, met the dressed up, spit and polish Marines. She screamed and screamed and screamed some more . . . but they wouldn't go away. I wonder what the neighbors thought.

When I got there, tragically late, but blameless in my mind, I felt as if the Marines had compounded the situation unnecessarily. Kitty was inconsolable so my parents filled me in. Well-l-l . . . she just never was the same person again. Three more very troubled marriages, periodic bouts with alcoholism (I'd help her out when she or the Department or her fourth husband called on me) and, finally, a drawn out death from pancreatic cancer ends this sad tale, almost.

Sgt. George William Storz's name is on the Viet Nam Memorial at the Marin County Civic Center as well as the one in Washington (Panel 43E, Line 062).

On the anniversary of George' ultimate sacrifice for his country, his buddies and the Corps, their son enlisted in the Marine Corps. It was another cruel but unintended assault on my sister's psyche. Now, years later, he still struggles with Gulf War syndrome.

Semper Fi, Guys . . .

# Mean, Bad Bill "D"

Bill "D" was a mean, nasty, alcoholic, wife-abusing, son of a bitch, especially when he was drinking hard. Other than that, he was a rather pleasant guy, when sober, with whom to chat.

One long evening at their home in Woodacre when he had been vocally and physically abusing his wife, she picked up a baseball bat and threatened to bean him with it. He told her she wouldn't dare (use it against him) and went for her again. She took a mighty swing and split his scalp with a glancing wild whack that laid it wide open,

Case # ᘔ3S07

[Turn page upside-down to reveal *real* Case #]

maybe four or five inches. He was unconscious on the blood-saturated sofa when I got there; splatters were here and there on the walls and floor and the room looked like a mild tornado had ripped through it. I wrapped up his head with a Kotex pad

47

under layers of gauze, cuffed him up and drove to the hospital at routine speed.

Back then, we didn't necessarily call for an ambulance, with the attendants having merely Advanced First Aid qualifications. EMT's and the more highly trained Paramedics were just becoming integral to fire departments and ours didn't have any yet. Besides, this S.O.B. was under arrest and it would be a waste of good manpower and equipment.

X-rays showed that his skull (fortunately for him, at least) was not fractured; also, there were no immediate signs of a compromising concussion. The jagged edges of the torn skin were curled under opposing parts due to the single, foul ball "strike" by his wife, who had finally stood up to the plate. The skin had to be pulled apart and the hair extracted and shaved off before he was stitched up without anesthesia. He probably didn't feel much pain anyway, still being highly intoxicated.

That particular Emergency Room doctor was known to be quite unsympathetic toward some of his patients for whom he had a Hippocratic Oath duty to treat to the best of his ability. That, to him, did not necessarily include respect or patience for wife beaters or, *even more especially,* baby rapists and those whom had assaulted police officers. I'm not sure about husband-beaters.

I kind of liked his attitude, and so did most of the nurses who worked with him. I watched with a sense of neutral detachment while having thoughts of admiration for his wife because she finally took direct and positive action to protect herself.

I always responded to calls for any service as quickly as reasonably possible and as circumstances dictated but, sometimes, direct action is more effectively efficient and protective than dialing 9-1-1, especially in rural areas where a long response time can be downright deadly.

After he was patched up and cleared for release, I took him to Jail where he belonged. Later on, he was either convicted or plead guilty to felony spousal abuse—forgot which one and what sentence he got.

Several weeks later, we bumped into each other. He was "clean and sober" and I asked him how he'd been doing. He knew damned well I wasn't talking about his head wound. He wryly commented, with an embarrassed yet friendly grin, that he thought he'd finally learned his lesson, and then some!

Y'know? They stayed together and we never had another call to their home.

# Gut-Shot

Deputy John Forsdal was a friend of mine. We'd had dinner together a couple of times.

He carried a "Buck" folding knife on his Sam Brown belt, as many of us did—not only as a defensive weapon but also as a first aid tool, to cut a seat belt, to get through the clothing of a lacerated body of an accident victim.

He'd been dispatched to a "civil dispute—"keep the peace" detail in Sleepy Hollow, an unincorporated area of San Anselmo. The husband and wife had been having their difficulties, as sometimes happens in relationships. The wife was moving out, at least temporarily, and was fearful that her husband might create a scene. Routine cop stuff.

Everything was going smoothly. WIFE got what she needed and was loading it in her car.

HUSBAND calls to John from the front porch to the street and says, "You have a phone call . . . it's the Sheriff's Department."

John walks to the door and is blasted by a shotgun. It blew out his belly and the underside of his left arm. His guts were hanging out and he couldn't get to his gun. He figured he was going to die but, with spirited determination and courage, tried to make a go of it. He couldn't reach his "Buck" knife on his left side and begged WIFE to get it for him so he could cut off his stomach and enable him to complete his mission. Gutsy guy (sort of, after this)! WIFE screams for help on John's radio . . . it comes.

When HUSBAND was booked, there was a cacophony of cheers from the inmates. **What sort of people are these?**

John received 50% disability retirement and was told he could sell tickets at the local movie theater to make up the difference. **Where's the justice? Where's the gratitude of the American public? Please tell me.**

# Bad-ass Bobby Frankel

He had a Thompson .45 caliber sub-machine gun and a couple of WW II "pineapple" hand grenades behind his front door, so I was told, but I couldn't jeopardize my informant at that time by obtaining a search warrant, because she lived across the courtyard from him in San Geronimo. Neither she nor I wanted to risk her life. I knew I'd figure out a different way, somehow.

He didn't trust me and I sure as Hell didn't trust him. Being a "speed freak" (addicted to methamphetamines) made him jumpy, sleepless, unpredictable and damned dangerous. Even so, we talked in my patrol car a couple of times after I assured him I wasn't tape recording our conversation. I even let him check out my brief cases and glove box, after I removed an extra handgun, a little Beretta "Bobcat" .25 caliber, semi-automatic with a flip-top barrel (not much of a man-stopper) . . .

His Mom, a widow, was a jewel in the little community of Forest Knolls and was mightily saddened by the life-course her son had taken. We talked some, but all of it was just sadness, disappointment and futility, tempered by her quite dignity. She thanked me for some of the good stuff that I had done with and for others . . .

I'd helped send him to prison. Earlier on, he'd had his jaw broken in three places with one punch by a good friend of mine when he'd gotten too far out of line. It had to be wired up for a while—he learned, then forgot, that he shouldn't shoot off his mouth so much because someone might come along and shut it up for him. Later on, he had an arm torn off in an industrial accident at a sugar factory up North somewhere, but this is the tale I want to share with you now . . .

Now a Sergeant, assigned to the Jail, I was in the process of being divorced: alone and lonely; sexually unsatisfied; longing for the loving touch and sympathetic conversation with a sensual and understanding woman; depressed to the point of seriously considering suicide. My hand literally itched for the grip of my off-duty Walther PP, 7.65mm. It was a valuable WW II German souvenir, issued to Nazi Postal Agents, according to its markings, and worth twice the price of one not so marked.

I really didn't give a damn about anything except my young son, Zachary. Concern for him, should I be gone forever, was my minimal deterrent. I didn't know where I was going in my life or if I was going to be able to "keep on keepin' on."

Roseanna, the not-so-bright daughter of one of my very best confidential informants, called me around 9:00 PM at my home up in the Penngrove foothills in Sonoma County (just North of Marin) from the pay phone outside the Forest Knolls Lodge. Bobby had put a pistol to her head and was threatening to kill her because of him losing custody of his kids due to his imprisonment. He correctly suspected that her Mom, my C.I., was largely responsible.

He was still inside the tavern, just yards away. I told her that I'd be right down but to get the Hell out of the area—go home or, better yet, to a friend's house, since she lived with her Mom in the same four-unit complex as Bobby, directly across the driveway. Somebody had shot a few rounds into their tiny bungalow, narrowly missing my C.I., and it had come from either the driveway or Bobby's unit. Take a guess.

My normal procedure would have been to tell her to call the Sheriff's Department or that I would call them for her. This was personal, though, and it was *my* call! Roseanna was not going to die tonight is I could help it.

I loaded up with several firearms including a "Hi-Standard" .22 magnum two-shot derringer with hollow-point bullets. Firing that handy palm-sized back-up gun at night would project a red muzzle blast maybe a nine inches long. At close range—maybe 10 feet—the twin over & under barrels aligned so that they would crisscross vertically by about a foot. I'd practiced with it several times, with my index finger along the flat-barreled side pointing at the target, while using my middle finger on the trigger. Deadly little sucker! They're illegal in Ultra-liberal California now . . .

I also threw in my M-1 .30 cal. military carbine with three 30-round clips taped together side by side with the center one upside down;

tucked my Walther inside my belt; and left for perhaps a destiny with death in Forest Knolls. Not so strangely, I felt okay about that.

My solitary mission that night was undoubtedly fueled by anger and resentment that a simple-minded meth-addicted daughter of a trusted and valuable informant had been threatened by a ruthless, good-for-nothing-but-crime bastard in the community that used to be part of my beat. He'd been a pesky, painful thorn in my foot for *way* too long.

I was mildly lubricated by my friend from Tennessee, John Barleycorn. I never lacked for courage, with or without booze, but sometimes I shook with fear or trembled in anticipation of adrenalin-infused pending violence. I actually came to welcome the latter, knowing from past experiences that my reactions would be like greased lightning. This night was different, though.

Speeding down Highway 101 in my little Chevy Nova II to Greenbrae and Kentfield, then out about 11 miles of residential Sir Francis Drake Blvd., I was there within about 45 minutes after the call. Under normal daytime conditions, it would have taken over an hour just to make the 45 miles, let alone my "prep" time."

I noticed a patrol car parked at the nearby San Geronimo Valley grade school and swung in. Paul S. was there with a Reserve Deputy, his brother-in-law, Bob G.

I told them that I had to take care of some personal business with a bad guy at the tavern and asked them to come bail me out in ten minutes if I didn't return.

Bobby was in the back room, playing pool. There were maybe seven men and a couple of low-life women in that small, smoky, sweat-and-urine-stinky room that jutted out over Papermill Creek. The walls seemed to be permeated with the barroom stench. More than once when I had walked in there, bad guys who may or may not have been "wanted" had bailed out the window and on to the rocks below.

I asked the bartender, one of Roseanna's three brothers, to tell Bobby that I wanted to talk with him. Bobby's insolent reply was, "If Travis wants to talk with me, tell him to come back here, *if he's not yellow.*"

I wasn't and I did, holding my derringer in my jacket pocket, ready to blow him to Hell where he truly belonged if he pulled his gun on me.

I walked back and confronted him, looking him squarely in the eyes, and advised him quietly that if anything happened to any of my friends, he would get the same, in spades. "Friends!", he shouted, about six inches in front of me, his spittle sprinkling my face, "What kind of your 'friends' send me to prison and take my kids away from me?" Near my right side, someone yelled, "Shut the fuck up, Frankel," then a beefy fist flew close by my nose in seemingly slow motion, as in a dream or the nightmares I had occasionally. I wondered, "Where in Hell did *that* come from—how'd he miss me?" It had come from one of Roseanna's brothers; I think the one whose life I had saved by sticking my thumb in his carotid artery after a bad wreck in Woodacre. Bobby disappeared from my view but came up on the other side of the pool table. Then the pool balls began to fly in all directions, not necessarily at me, and I saw at least one pool stick being broken over the table edge, to be used as a short club.

It was time for me to "get out of Dodge" and let the dust settle. I walked casually past the bar, mindful that my backside was unprotected, but still clutching my concealed derringer. As I pushed open the front door, the duty Sergeant, Jim R., and the two Deputies slammed it back at me as they rushed inside to rescue me. "Let's get out of here, it's over," I told them. I left quickly to avoid explanations and, quite frankly, I don't know how much of the pandemonium they witnessed or what they did about it, if anything.

Bobby and the others had gotten my message and that was all I cared about.

Me, I went home, content for the time being, and fell into a deeply satisfied sleep.

I never heard a word from anyone about my "bar visit" with Bobby—the Brass, the Sergeant, the Deputies, the bartender or the tavern owner.

# Captain Hemorrhoid

Most of us in the local law enforcement community referred to him as "that asshole." My Sergeant corrected me one day: an asshole has a useful purpose, that of excretion. A hemorrhoid is useless, the closest thing to an asshole and irritating as Hell. His revised moniker became "Captain Hemorrhoid."

He was dishonorable. He flagrantly violated the Law Enforcement Code of Ethics. When I was a rookie, working in the old San Rafael Jail in the basement of the stately, turn-of-the century Court House (subsequently torched and destroyed), there was a public-service outreach to have folks turn in handguns which subsequently would be taken out on San Francisco Bay and dumped. An attractive widow brought in an exquisite matched pair of single-shot dueling pistols in a walnut case (with bullet molds, cleaning rods, and a powder flask), probably worth at that time maybe $5,000, today maybe ten times that. Where do you suppose they ended up? He also had a large quantity of knives, previously stored in the evidence locker.

In a drunken nighttime episode, he was involved in a hit-run injury accident with his County-owned car and, in a cowardly manner, left the scene and went home. He later plead "*nolo contendere*," avoiding criminal charges.

He once evacuated the Civic Center ($10,000 per hour in lost wages at the time) on his evaluation that the cover of a Tampax dispenser in a toilet bowl was likely a bomb. He later kicked a "suspicious" Christmas gift to ascertain if it would explode, thus saving the County $10,000.

During a party at the San Geronimo Golf Course, he was so obnoxious that a guest punched him out.

He couldn't walk by a mirror or even a window which would cast his reflection without glancing at himself, his pompadour grandiosely fluffed and stiff with hair spray.

Once we really butted heads over a point of relatively new law with which I was mandated to comply. He had no idea of its passage. I became insubordinate, in his mind, with my insistence that I adhere to the law. He summoned me to the Undersheriff's office where I was asked why the Captain and I could not get along. I looked at the Captain and replied, "Because he's a thief and a liar and I don't trust or respect him."

There was a very pregnant silence, then I was dismissed. There was no further action, not a single word.

I suspect that he may have had something on the Sheriff, who had ties with La Cosa Nostra.

Maybe I should not be so resentful and critical of a deceased person, but he brought disrespect to our Department and Marin County law enforcement.

What a jerk! Can you blame me for my disappointment?

# Sunday Morning Ride on the Bubble-gum Machine

Back in the 60's, we had big bulky emergency lights and sirens that slowed down top speed considerably. Not only that, but because when all of the equipment was activated on long Code 3 runs, there would be a tremendous drain on the standard battery. If there weren't many cars on the road, and I was in an area of relatively high visibility, I wouldn't use my siren at night because of the extra drain that it created.

I vividly recall one night, screaming West down Sir Francis Drake Blvd. in the San Geronimo Valley, just past the Lagunitas Store. I was coming up on Dead Man's Curve with its huge Redwood tree that had been the last thing many a driver saw in his life. I leaned on the horn ring that activated the siren when the red lights were on, but the damn headlights dimmed so suddenly that I could barely see the road. I managed the curve but vowed to remember that precaution in the future.

The photograph is of an early 60's Plymouth high-performance Fury, a couple of years before my time. It is an original Marin County Sheriff's patrol car, lovingly and accurately restored by the son of deceased Sergeant Ed McKamey, after reclaiming it from a junk yard several years ago. The photograph was taken in 2011 at the edge of Stafford Lake near Novato, during a lavish picnic hosted by the Deputy Sheriffs Association. It was in honor of one of our own, slain in the line of duty. The bittersweet gathering helped us in the grief recovery process, but that's another chapter.

One early Saturday morning around 1:45 AM when I was responsible for both my own beat in The Valley as well as the adjoining one in Pt. Reyes Station (which covered the majority of West Marin on both sides of Tomales Bay) I was out by Limantour Spit near Drake's Bay Estero when Sergeant McKamey dispatched me to a barking dog complaint in Woodacre. I told him my location (about 35 miles away and 40 minutes driving time) and asked him if he could have the Kentfield area Deputy handle it. From the Western edge of that beat, it would have taken about 10 minutes. His terse response: "Negative!" I got the idea that maybe he thought that we Resident Deputies were a bunch of *prima donnas* as "Lieutenant Deadfoot" had once called us but, no matter, I wasn't doing anything but trying to keep both beats clean so, if that's the way he wants it, I'll just do it. "10-4, en route." Maybe the Area II Deputy was tied up on something more important. Most of the time, I couldn't hear the radio traffic between the other Deputies "over the hill."

I arrived at the location and reawakened the lady complainant to take a belated report. She was *not* a Happy Camper. I was perversely satisfied, though, knowing that if any bovine excrement hit the proverbial fan, it would splatter on the duty Sergeant, not on me.

The first car assigned to me was also a Plymouth, an old '64 Belvedere with 100,000 miles on the odometer, a wobbly front end and nearly bald tires. I inherited it from Deputy Billy Wallace, whom I was replacing. Instead of the twin whirly-gigs on top like the one above, it had only one rotating red light plus a steady red one, as required by law. It was housed in a rounded dome shape, taller than wide, and we commonly referred to it as "the Bubble-gum machine."

Bright and early on a Sunday morning before early masses or other church services, and after hitting the sack around 3:00 AM, I was dispatched to back up Joe Dentoni, a relatively new Deputy, working the Pt. Reyes beat. Seems there was a naked man acting a wee bit strange in the middle of the main drag of Pt. Reyes Station, Highway One, in front of the Western Saloon.

As Joe approached him in his patrol car with his emergency lights on (he told me later), WEIRDO turned his back and spread his butt cheeks, as if inviting the vehicle to sodomize him.

As I rolled around Nicasio Reservoir, Joe told me that the guy had jumped up on the car roof and had his legs wrapped around the bubble machine. Joe asked me, "What should I do? What's your E.T.A.?"

I slammed down the accelerator and told him I'd be there in about five minutes and to just drive slowly around town on the side roads to keep him entertained until I arrived. We met at the old combination Courtroom and Substation building next to the firehouse, grabbed him by whatever we could reach and dragged him to the narrow side walk.

He had a mighty proud erection and, as we were struggling to get handcuffs on him, he was trying to fornicate one of the spaces in the sidewalk. After a bit of a tussle, we got him in handcuffs and leg irons (no protective "cages" then). Joe drove him into the Crisis Center at Marin General Hospital and gave the rundown to the psychiatric folks. Lots of disbelief, then giggles and guffaws.

Never did find out what sort of drug he was on, maybe L.S.D., Angel Dust or mushrooms? Who knows? For sure, I pitied his poor pecker!

# Danny Joe, Stupid Thief

He'd been ripping off houses in West Marin for several months, probably to support a drug habit.

My friend, Constable Mike McLean, assigned to the Justice Court, and also a Special Deputy Sheriff, had distributed "Wanted" posters with his photo and a whopping $5.00 in good old U. S. dollars for his arrest and conviction.

Stupid Danny Joe had a sixteen-foot stake-side Ford truck, loaded with loot from several burglaries. I was hunting him and one dark night found his truck and his girlfriend in front of the Lagunitas post office. They knew they were in deep doo-doo. I moved off a way and watched. She drove off after I had told her not to drive since she didn't have a license. I heard a scream. Dumb-shit Danny had crawled under the bed, straddled the drive shaft and, with his shoulder-length hair, got tangled up as it spun. I followed at their slow pace, sounding my siren. He dropped off, ran like a rabbit down the embankment, dove into a blackberry patch and hid. Ouch! I can't to this day figure how he made it home to a remotely located cabin maybe half a mile away. His girlfriend got out of the cab and walked home after a stern warning not to drive anymore.

I hung around for a while, waiting for him to surface. After a while, I busted in their front door without knocking (in "fresh pursuit of a fleeing felon"). He was soaking his battered, scratched and bloody body, including his somewhat hairless scalp, in the bathtub.

I hooked him and booked him over the strenuous and frantic objections of his girlfriend. My partner had the burdened flatbed towed and stored "over the Hill." It was forfeited and most of his ill-gotten gains were claimed by their owners after we displayed them in a local school gym.

A few weeks later, with my ankle broken in a skiing wreck, I led a squad of narcotics officers to his place during a county-wide coordinated execution of search warrants. He had made several sales of methamphetamine to one of our undercover guys. I threw away my crutches as I hobbled up the driveway. Major seizure. Hooked and booked again. Dumb sombitch . . .

# Big Rock Rape

"1-L-17—Just received a report of a forcible rape and sodomy at Big Rock." "10-4, enroute from Nicasio—vehicle description?"

Big Rock is a boulder maybe 70 feet high at the crest of Lucas Valley Road which meanders from the central corridor of Highway 101 in East Marin to its end at Nicasio Valley Road, 10.5 miles long. Residential, then rural, past George Lucas' "Skywalker Ranch," through the redwoods (with a carved redwood statue of a grizzly bear, past the home of a friend whom I had taken on his final journey—where we had a stand-off with an armed kidnap suspect a few years before. He'd given me fifty bucks when my infant son died: said, "Go piss it away." I figured he'd had a similar loss but didn't think he wanted me to inquire further. Sometimes, silence in the company of a good friend who understands is the most compassionate comforter.

I snapped out of those thoughts as I saw the suspect vehicle coming head-on. I turned on my emergency lights, slowing almost to a stop, straddling the center line. The S.O.B. accelerated and swerved around me. "You're pissing me off! And I'm going to get you, whatever it takes." No back-up; I didn't care. Did a high-speed reverse 180-degree spin and took off after those bastards who ignored my authority. Nobody messes with me in West Marin!

Caught up with 'em on Nicasio Valley Road—for some reason, they gave up. They had the audacity to claim that there was another perpetrator who had jumped out and run away toward a couple of nearby houses. I hooked them up (hands to hands around a utility pole, thankful that I carried two sets of handcuffs). I checked around the houses and concluded that they were just pulling my chain, maybe to gain time to free themselves.

The young lady had wisely taken part of a matchbook cover from inside the car and, guess what? You got it—the matching half was in the pocket of one of bad brothers. This was before DNA came on scene so it was pretty good stuff. Other evidence from the car and the victim, including a line-up, cinched the case. I imagine that she went to a doctor for follow-up care, but we didn't have forensic "rape kits' for prosecution purposes then.

PRISON! Did my job and proud of it. VERY impressed with the young lady!

# Guts on the Barroom Floor

"Piss on 'em and stuff 'em back in" was what I was taught about exposed intestines as a Signalman in the U. S. Naval Reserve. It is the best, most available "solution" to prevent the innards from adhering together and requiring subsequent complicated surgery.

There was a nighttime brawl going on at the Forest Knolls Lodge (now the Papermill Creek Saloon) but I was thirteen miles away on a mail run at the "Blue Roof Inn," the Marin County Civic Center and Hall of Justice, the only government building designed by the late Frank Lloyd Wright.

Normally, it would take about a half-hour to get there; I screamed past the lollygagging ambulance in San Anselmo and contemplated on the next morning's headlines: "Local deputy urinates on stabbing victim." I marvel at my brain's capacity to process my esoteric thoughts as I drive at breakneck speed.

I made it in about fifteen minutes. Sure enough, there he lay. He had it coming to him. He'd been making a fool of himself, got challenged, tried to leave in his truck but another patron rammed him. How he ended up back in the tavern was never clear to me. It didn't matter.

He survived.

# O.S.S. Agent, Forensic Artist & Patch Designer

**Ed Mauberret** and my mentor, Ken Irving, were both agents of the Office of Strategic Services, the predecessor of the Central Intelligence Agency (C. I. A.) during the Second World War. Another friend who, with his wife, bought a home from me, was one of our spies with the State Department. He was so deeply underground in Germany that, in order to receive his pension that he so richly deserved, he had to provide the license plate number of an ammunition truck traversing Nazi Berlin 1944. I had his strongbox for several years.

I cannot possibly compare myself to such heroic contributors and protectors of our society . . . but they *were* my friends—and now they all of them are gone. And so I honor one of them here.

Ed Mauberret knew well how to operate a Thompson .45 caliber submachine gun but his style surprised me down at the range one day as I was practicing for an upcoming pistol match. He placed the stock horizontally between his thighs and, very accurately, punctured the man-silhouette target with 15 rounds.

Like many of us in our chosen professions, we acquire troublesome burdens. Some are never lifted. Those choices were ours.

Ed Mauberret designed the highly coveted shoulder patch, which is also incorporated into the Marin County Sheriff's Department logos. I've been recently told that the design concept and original draft were conceived by a jail inmate. I still stay in touch with Ed's widow.

He was so highly skilled in interviewing victims and witnesses to crimes that he one time created a drawing of a suspect that strongly resembled a photograph later taken during the suspect's booking process.

He offered to do a painting for the cover of this book you are now perusing, but his time ran out.

# The Shadows

"The Shadows," deep in the ancient, towering redwoods of Nicasio, with a seasonal creek, is almost a sacred place. It is also a place of joyous celebrations. The Sheriff's Department had been having annual parties there since I was a rookie, with live Country &Western music, steaks, baked potatoes and salads and supportive camaraderie. It was where we could exuberantly or quietly shed our burdens with fellow peace officers and mates, knowing that we were secure among those who understand what we do and why we do it.

On one of those barbequed evenings, as the liquor took its effect with its reduction of inhibitions, some long simmering resentments emerged. Captain Hemorrhoid made a blatantly sexual pass toward a buddy's wife and got decked with a punch to the jaw. Served him right, but it was time to settle things down.

About twenty of the guys and gals retired to our home on a nearby ranch for an early morning breakfast of spicy *huevos rancheros* with all of the trimmings.

My longtime partner and Air Force veteran, Russ, wore a "Fifty Mission Crush" hat (from WW II aviation lore) with the sides flopped down. The brass strongly disapproved of it so we decided that it was time to "retire" it. Actually, we "terminated" it. We tossed it up into the night sky several times and shot at it with our revolvers with no luck. I got my 12-guage Remington Model 870 riot shotgun out of the patrol car and blew a hole in that hat so it could never be used again. Russ seemed okay with it.

That same evening, the infamous MCDAB gang of five (Marin County Drug Abuse Bureau) drove off the cliff at Big Rock on Lucas Valley Road. They were so well lubricated that none were seriously injured. The squad was subsequently disbanded under pressure from the public and subsequent

70

defunding by the Board of Supervisors. That was the apparent end of our traditions at "The Shadows."

Several years later, the morale of the Sheriff's Office was on serious wane. Part of the problem was that many of the newer deputies could not afford to live in the affluent, high-priced real estate of Marin and did not have any particular devotion or loyalty to it. Some on Patrol had no idea how to respond to various areas of West Marin, never having taken the time to familiarize themselves. Back up? Forget it!

Something needed to be done!

I decided to reinstate "The Shadows" experience in a major way and it was going to be a doozy.

Wrap your mind around this, if you will: A healing and stimulating cohesive celebration that enabled all three shifts of the Sheriff's Department to enjoy.

My second wife, Susan, had left me for a while, so I was dallying around with other women for the comforting and supportive satisfactions most men need. I enlisted some of them for the pending project.

On-duty deputies solicited merchants for donations as prizes and many contributed willingly—an 18-speed bicycle, cases of motor oil, dinners at local hostelries. It seemed right at the time. Today, it wouldn't fly.

The "tickets" I created were on full page card stock with tear-off stubs for complementary drinks and a list of all of the donated prizes on the reverse side. We easily sold over 300, with guests including the District Attorney, Probation and Public Defenders Offices and private citizens.

Some old redwood barn board and vivid paint became signs. The outhouses were "Stallions" and "Mares." The "Red Eye Saloon" hung over the bar. One of my heroes, a Marine Corps Sgt., Deputy Richard "Gunny" Richmond was presiding.

It was an all-day event that began at noon with sack races, badminton, hot dogs, s'mores (hot marshmallows and Hershey chocolate on Graham crackers) and swimming for the

71

kids. It flowed into the late afternoon as the guys and gals from Dayshift were arriving.

Deputy "Laura" challenged me as her Sergeant and criticized the way I ran my shifts. Her disrespect was not acceptable to me. I told her that if she didn't retract it, I would toss her into a nearby refuse dumpster. She refused. She got dumped. I don't think she's ever gotten over it.

We had borrowed a "dunk tank" from the local Lion's Club and filled it with chilly spring water from Rancho Nicasio. "Victims" included our Undersheriff, Hank Ingwersen and two judges (one who later became my erstwhile father-in-law) and one more whom I have forgotten, maybe the D.A. Poor Hank—every time he got dunked, someone gave him a shot of brandy. By four that afternoon, that good sport could barely stand unassisted. His loving and tolerant wife, with our assistance, loaded him into their car and home they went.

Hank died a few years later. His funeral at Mission San Rafael was reminiscent of JFK's, with a horse-drawn, glass-windowed hearse followed by a riderless horse with reverse-turned boots in the stirrups. He went out in style.

I had made an inquiry and request of George Lucas' wife, Marcia (before they divorced) as to whether Darth Vader, the villain of Star Wars, might make a guest appearance to further liven up the festivities for the kids. A day later, all was in place, with the proviso that a uniformed deputy had to accompany Darth at all times. Deputy Ralph Pfeifer, the miraculous survivor of bloody havoc in South East Asia, was my choice. "Darth" and his sister flew up from Southern California. Around two in the afternoon, there he stood on the dance floor, breathing in that ominous, guttural tone and threatening the youngsters to be good.

A local liquor store had fronted us many cases of soda pop, wine and hard liquor, allowing us to return any unused product. Toby's Feed Barn in Pt. Reyes Station loaned us several bales of straw for additional seating. The Sheriff granted us the use of an officially marked utility van and we loaded that sucker to its max, with the beverages inside and the straw bales on top. "Danny Dollar and the Bourbon Cowboys" provided the evening tunes.

As the evening wore happily on, Anita, one of my lady friends, a dispatcher who had to report for duty at midnight, lured me into the woods for passionate and intimate fondling. She had been jockeying all night against "Tatiana," for my affectionate attention. "Tatiana," a sensuous, wide-hipped, large-breasted, full-lipped black vixen would follow me home for a glorious night.

The next morning, it was back to **The Shadows** to make everything right again. It was a challenge, but thanks to Deputy "Conk," we got 'er done.

**Me and Deputy "Conk"—the morning after**

# "The Quick and the Dead"

I can't drive around much of my old Valley beat more than three of four miles at a stretch without going by a spot where someone died or was rescued. Here's a smattering of some of the more memorable ones:

Saturday morning about 8:30 in Nicasio, after being up 'til the wee hours that morning, all pooped out and, contrary to my usual practice, without much gas in my tank. The guys at the Woodacre firehouse didn't appreciate being disturbed late. Dispatch calls. Weldon, some baby got into the medicine cabinet in Lagunitas and consumed most of the pills—no Ipecac syrup to induce vomiting—the Doctor told Mom that 15 minutes was about max time. I bolted from bed, yanked on a uniform shirt, some grungy, woodcutting Levis and slipped into a handy pair of dairy boots. Took the outside stairs in three bounds, cranked up the car, hit the lights and kept it floorboarded most of the way to Lagunitas; couldn't find the latch to the six-foot gate so rolled over it. Mom and baby there, strapped both down tight as I could in the front seat and told them to hang on—it's going to be a fast ride. Slid into the Forest Knolls station for a couple gallons of gas and yelled that I'd be back later to pay.

Radioed Dispatch to have Fairfax, San Anselmo, Ross, Kentfield Fire know that I'd be coming through *fast!* Bless 'em, every single major intersection was blocked off but not Butterfield Road in San Anselmo. On the downhill right curve, a car was turning into the intersection, saw us roaring down on him; he floored it and ended up high on the church lawn. Good man! We were airborne for about 11 feet. Mom let out a loud, panic-filled gasp and on we roared past Sir Francis Drake High School, through the old railroad "Hub" in San Anselmo, screaming through upscale Ross into Kentfield and past the college, to Greenbrae and Marin General Hospital. They were waiting for us as we skidded to a stop at the Emergency Room entrance. Baby was pumped out and survived. Back home to

75

write my report (with my heart beating normally again) I called dispatch for times. Thirteen minutes flat from receiving the call to 10-7 at the hospital! A recheck of the radio log confirmed it. Hard to believe, still.

* * *

Old "Cat Lady" living in a dank house on Redwood Drive in Woodacre. No one had seen her in days. She was dead, alright, and the cats didn't have any food except her. When the Coroner got there, I helped put her in a rubberized body bag. Her forearm skin slipped off as a pulled her off the bed. Uniform stripped off outdoors at home, then to the cleaners in a plastic garbage bag. It still stunk.

* * *

Another old lady living a few houses away had a warning signal to her neighbors who took daily walks by her place: If she was alive and kicking, the front window shade would be up by 9:00 AM. It hadn't been up for three days when I got the call. Damn! Not another one . . . I couldn't find a quick way inside without breaking something, so I bashed in the front door—should have gone through a window—cheaper. A blast of very hot air hit me—must have been over 100 degrees in there. This wasn't going to be pretty. Found her in bed, barely conscious. She had a bad bout with a nasty flu bug. I got her going again and had an ambulance get her to the hospital for rehydration and eventual recovery. A couple of days later and angry, she called up the Brass and wanted me to reimburse her for her busted door. Oh well . . .

* * *

Ten at night, unresponsive baby in a crib, SFD Blvd. in Forest Knolls. Mental check list on CPR while en route Code 3. Knocked on the front door, no response. Banged on the front door, still nothing, door locked. Out comes my baton and I thumped the door good. Teary eyed young Mom comes to the door, thinks the baby is gone, apologizes for her husband who had to shoot up some heroin before continuing down this sad road. Baby was clearly dead, with just a little nasal effluent. Looks like S.I.D.S. (Sudden Infant Death Syndrome) to me. I poked around a little; talked a little; observed everything I thought might be important but didn't bother with a narcotics investigation; called for the Coroner; sent a copy of my report to the Dicks and to Child Protective Services. Not much else I could or wanted to do. Poor kids, all three of them . . .

\* \* \*

Dead man; a mean, nasty, brutal dope dealer, killed by an intentional overdose, dumped in a roadside ditch above Fairfax on the indirect road to Bolinas on the Coast. Not much time spent by me or any others investigating this one. Good riddance . . .

\* \* \*

Another dope deal body dump—down in the seasonal creek, opposite the turnout just West of Big Rock on Lucas Valley Road. Probably killed up near his home in Tomales by the Bay. Head caved way in, most likely with a crowbar. The Detective Bureau handled that one—I think they developed a suspect but I don't remember if any arrest was made.

\* \* \*

Elderly gentleman in Forest Knolls, not seen for a few days, he'd been cooking under an electric blanket turned on high. Not pleasant. Some of his gun collection was missing, probably taken by the low-life neighbor who reported finding him. I couldn't make a case of it.

\* \* \*

Cold, dark, foggy early evening in Pt. Reyes Station. Several of us, including town folks, had heard a small plane circling low overhead then heading away into the night. The pilot, his young wife and infant child had flown down the coast from Oregon, after ignoring warnings about heavy fog around San Francisco Bay. They found a hillside up on Mt. Vision in Inverness after apparently flying low, visually without adequate instrumentation. Following the coast line Southward, they came upon narrow, nine-mile long Tomales Bay and turned left, ending up at end of it at Pt. Reyes Station. Heading South again, they met their destiny. The recovery was in steep, difficult terrain. The mental difficulties, the stupidity of it all, was difficult, too. Their kid was a cute, innocent cherub, now an angel. At least they're all together still . . .

* * *

Early milking time at the Genazzi Ranch in Nicasio. Suicide—maybe murder. I'd had two bowls of spicy *chili con carne* the night before and my stomach was more than a tad queasy. Buck pointed to the bunk house across the sloppy barnyard. I slipped into my dairy boots and waded through the smelly manure, urine and muddy slop. My stomach and bowels really churned up when I entered the hot confines of the tiny structure. Slowly and deliberately, I surveyed the scene, which was somewhat strange. He had obviously been shot in or on his bunk, but his body was laying perpendicular to the bed on the rough plank floor. His bullet perforated head was bracketed by a pair of Indian moccasins, as if carefully, perhaps respectfully, placed there. His bunkmate wasn't much help—he spoke very limited English and was most likely an illegal immigrant. Yearning for a bathroom to clear my system, I snapped several pictures and waited for the Coroner and the "meat wagon." He wasn't a very happy camper, either.

The victim had typical Mexican features but his heritage and belief systems were predominantly Native American—Southwestern tribe of some sort. I cogitated on the circumstances for several hours, wondering if there were any significance to the placement of the moccasins. I embarked on a telephonic journey with several Native American resources but no one was able to come up with a verifiable confirmation of my theory that someone had symbolically provided him with foot protection for his journey to the "Happy Hunting Grounds." Not much more I could do . . .

\* \* \*

Chuck was a 19-year-old kid and petty thief—hubcaps, wheels, high-end stereo gear; he dabbled in marijuana sales and, later, heroin. He had a weight-lifting crime buddy, strong as an ox. They would unbolt a set of fancy mag wheels, then his buddy would lift up each side of the car in turn, while Chuck would remove the tires and rims.

I'd been down with some local kids at the Woodacre Improvement Club around curfew time when his '65 Dodge 440 Charger came into the lot, spun a 180 and peeled out—spraying gravel and leaving a long stripe of dual tire marks ("Positraction," too). I hopped in my Patrol car, put on my lap belt and took off in hot pursuit. About a quarter of a mile down Redwood Drive, alongside a creek, I came across Chuck's cherished ride, pretty well totaled out. He was GOA and I didn't feel inclined to get messed up looking for him in the trees and blackberry bushes. Anyway, I couldn't prove that he was the driver who ran off into the woods of Woodacre but figured he'd already paid a dear price.

I'd warned him, directly and through his dubious "friends," that he was heading for a big fall. He didn't listen. Several months later, fortunately on my days off, his friends poured his inert body through the bunkhouse window at the LaFranchi Ranch where he died from an accidental overdose of heroin. "You can lead a horse to water, but you can't make him drink." He wasn't a bad kid, just bull-headed . . .

Lots more, but you get the picture.

# Limantour Spit, Spacebound

It was one of those weeks when I had most of West Marin as my beat. Others were injured, on their days off or rejuvenating on vacation.

Dutifully, I was all over the back roads, poking around, quietly doing my patrol. Sometimes, Dispatch lost track of my comings and goings, especially when they changed shifts. I was usually on the road at different times around the clock. When Dispatch called for "time and location" checks, I'd give 'em local landmarks like "Purple Cow Meadow," "Moon Hill," "The Bull Rushes," "Cow Hollow," "The Elephants" (a huge rock formation on the Coast) or "The Inkwell," a swimming hole in Papermill Creek. There would be an understandably quizzical pause, then simply "10-4." Most had no idea that I was actually telling them where I was and that, if I really needed a backup, one of my fellow Resident Deputies would know where to find me. Another consideration was that I didn't want the crooks who listened on scanners to know where I was.

One late night, I was 'way out on the Point Reyes peninsula, intending to check the parking lots of the Light House, Chimney Rock, Ten Mile Beach and Limantour Spit for anyone out of their element.

I found one.

He was sitting cross-legged in the middle of the two-lane road, maybe contemplating his navel or the brilliant starscape. I thought at first that he might be a feral pig, previously domestic, bedding down for the night, absorbing the warmth of the asphalt. They can grow to be huge, with four-inch deadly tusks. It's weird how these thoughts flow through my mind in times like this; but, on the other hand, they have contributed to my survival.

I blocked the roadway, turned on my flashing lights and cautiously approached this strange apparition.

He was from another planet, wild-eyed, sweating, disturbed, meditative . . . a jumble of confused humanity. I figured LSD or "Angel Dust" (an animal tranquilizer) . . . it didn't matter which. He needed to go to the Crisis Center

I coaxed him into my "Peerless" handcuffs and then into the back seat of the patrol car. We had no protective cages then and any timely backup was dubious at best.

As we started off for the maybe 65 mile ride to the Crisis Center, he roared like an African lion and lunged over the seat with his mouth wide open, obviously intent on devouring my right cheek.

Instinctively, my right elbow stuck him sharply, dead center in his forehead, temporarily stunning him in a major way. I carried a set of old San Quentin Prison leg-irons, an eight-foot length of chain and a pair of matching padlocks in my trunk. I hog-tied him and chained him to the amber light on the rear deck.

He bellowed like a bull elephant; wailed like a banshee; whimpered like an orphaned kitten; sobbed and cried as if he'd lost a parent or a child. Then he was silent. For a moment, I thought he may have died but, then, I could hear his labored breathing.

We arrived at the old Jail on Fourth Street about an hour and a half later where, in earlier days, those men condemned to death were hanged from the Court Floor and dropped down into the Jail. Later, that gallows became an elevator shaft, adjacent to our telephone switchboard operator. I stay in touch with one of those ladies, who later became a Deputy Sheriff.

"Spacebound" had sweated out almost all of his demons, at least for a while, so I had decided that Jail would be more appropriate than the Crisis Center.

I wanted to make sure that no one else would be endangered by this man, so I talked with him further.

He was all done. He apologized to me. Both of us were safe with each other. What had transpired in his twisted and

81

confused mind? Would he regain his sanity? I knew what went through my mind—I had survived once again!

Before going home after a very long night that included hand-writing my report, I checked the rear seat. It was saturated with the man's sweat, maybe urine, and it splashed in my face when I swatted it. I'm guessing that he had lost about a half-gallon of body fluids. It dried out a few days later but the stench lingered longer.

My wife, Mary Lou, was a special comfort that night.

# F.B.I. turns Red, WHITE and Blue

August 7[th,] 1970 was a very bad day. Judge Haley had his head blown off; his son-in-law, Gary Thomas (prosecuting the case, later becoming a Judge, himself), was permanently paralyzed from the waist down; and my juror friend was taken hostage, further traumatized as her sister later combed teeth out of her hair. Some lives ended justifiably, other lives were changed tragically forever. It was the "Marin County Shoot-out" to facilitate the release of George Jackson, with that Communist [*expletive*], Angela Davis (his lover) and Jonathan Jackson (his 17 year-old brother) the duplicitous accomplices, among many others.

*This* part of *that* story follows:

The Ford "Econoline" van used in the aborted escape attempt had been stored out at the County Corporation Yard in Nicasio. Several nights later, my partner Russ Hunt and I had responded to a report of four of five black males prowling within the Cyclone-fenced property. It was a dark and spooky night. Our anxiety levels were high and the adrenalin was flowing as we poked and peeked around the many trucks, other heavy equipment, culvert pipes and construction equipment. We all figured later that it was most likely an attempt to steal or torch the van, thus preventing further forensic investigations and its use in the forthcoming prosecutions. It failed, but we made no apprehensions that night.

A few days later, there was an abandoned pickup truck in nearby San Geronimo at the base of Moon Hill on Nicasio Valley Drive. Some good teenagers I knew very well (they had come to my rescue when I was fired) were snooping around in the bed of the truck and took home a suitcase containing several photographs, thinking they might determine the owner of the vehicle. Other motivations are unknown to me to this day. The most significant black and white snapshot was one of Lee Harvey Oswald, the purported "lone assassin" of President

John Fitzgerald Kennedy, standing with a rifle similar to the one recovered in Dallas, in a good-natured pose with the sister of Vice-President Lyndon Baines Johnson. Curious, no? I never saw that or other photos. My recollection is that Inspector Ken Irving had received them and turned them over to the local F. B. I. Supervising Agent in San Rafael. My relating this tale is hearsay, at best.

Skip forward another eight or ten years, if you will. One of those teenagers was now a young lady student at Santa Rosa Junior College, attending a class in the Administration of Justice (studying to become a police officer). Her instructor was an F.B.I. agent, retired, as I recall these many years later. She brought up this event in her earlier life to the class at large and, as she told me later that evening, the instructor blanched, with the color of his face quickly draining.

He called her up to his desk and told her that under no circumstance should she ever mention this subject again, to anyone! Her life, and the lives of her family, could be in serious jeopardy.

Later events, including Watergate, the Clinton years of many mysterious deaths, the new awareness of the New World Order, Jekyll Island (off the Carolinas) planning sessions involving Kissinger, Rockefeller, the Bushes I & II, lend credence to my little friend's tale. New Orleans D. A. Jim Garrison had it right.

My suggestion is that you, The Reader, take heed that our Government may not have our own individual best interests in mind. It troubles me in my retirement years, as one sworn and still committed "To Protect and Serve" you.

# Big John's Colt Python

Most jumpers just look down at the swift, cold water for a few seconds, climb, roll or vault over the railing and start their freefall into oblivion. This poor sap had climbed up the large woven cable on the east side of the Golden Gate Bridge from mid-span and just stood there, looking down. He was out of reach but close enough to talk to. The commute traffic was at a dead stop, watching Big John, the Highway Patrol motorcycle officer, other cops, bystanders and bridge workers try to talk the man down.

Big John looked like Jonathan Winters, the rubbery-faced comedian; wide expressive countenance that usually had a wicked and mischievous grin on it but which could screw up into a menacing scowl if you antagonized him. He was maybe 5-foot-ten and 245 pounds—he dwarfed his Harley so that it resembled a Vespa motor scooter. He used to be a linebacker on a semi-pro football team, then became a city cop in Brisbane down on the Peninsula. Dissatisfied with the confinement of a small department, he lateraled to the Sheriff's Department and became a Resident Deputy in West Marin. The S/O didn't run motorcycles, though, and that's what John wanted to do. The C.H.P. brass got frustrated with him sometimes because he didn't follow a lot of their rules and wouldn't take any crap off them. At roll call, if they came up with some new procedure or policy or politically-influenced decision that didn't make sense, he'd screw on that lopsided grin, tilt his head a little to one side and tell 'em it wouldn't work or it was cockamamie B. S. and he wouldn't do it. They didn't like his insubordination, but usually had to agree with him. And they liked and respected him, to boot.

John carried a big Colt Python with a six-inch barrel and a shrouded ejector rod extending to the muzzle—you could spot one from 50 yards away. He wore it in a swivel clam-shell holster like Broderick Crawford wore in "Highway Patrol." A clam-shell sprang open at the front when you pushed a hidden button with your trigger finger—the trouble with them was that when you went to put the gun back, you had to use both hands. Made it kind of difficult when you were wresting with a bad guy trying to get the cuffs on—a one-armed paperhanger sort of situation.

We didn't have hostage negotiators or SWAT teams or Department chaplains back then. The Bridge was now a long parking lot, horns honking, people standing in the roadway—there was no easy resolution in sight.

So John did the only reasonable and prudent thing, duly photographed and reproduced on the front page of the Independent Journal the next day: He dragged out that long-barreled hogleg, pointed it straight and true to the would-be jumper and hollered up at him, "Get down off of there or I'll blow your 'frigging' head off!"

He did.

The traffic got back to normal as the poor guy went to the nut house.

Like Sinatra, Big John did it his way.

One early evening shortly after John retired, his big heart gave out on him as he was enjoying a hot tub in his back yard.

I miss the big, happy galoot . . .

# Heroic Deputy, Done In by a Bee and a Horse

Deputy Ralph was a survivor, big time. In South East Asia, sometimes Viet Nam, he was one of two survivors of a Company of 160 men. I cannot imagine the horror of slaughter he witnessed or how he existed on the ammo and food of dead foe and comrades. He had a cold, dead look in his eyes, yet went about our business in a workmanlike manner. He earned the respect and appreciation of the citizens we serve.

He'd had a troublesome relationship with his former lady. She was schizophrenic and depressed. One night, she shot herself, right through the heart. Ralph saved her life by plugging up the hole with his thumb until the regular paramedics arrived. He filled me in at the next morning's briefing.

The Marin Sheriff's Department had a formal policy forbidding the carry of back-up guns, but it was ignored by many. As a Deputy, I frequently had a .22 magnum Hi-Standard two-shot derringer tucked into my belt nighttimes, also a .25 Beretta in my briefcase. Ralph carried three guns, all of the time. Knowing of his experiences and my own practice as a Deputy and now a Sergeant, I let it lay.

We were at his home for a Halloween costume party—pretty gals were all around, skimpily, seductively and alluringly attired. Most were dispatchers or cop groupies. I was sitting on a couch with my eventual ex-wife and felt a lump underneath the cushion. Gun there, gun behind me, guns in the kitchen cabinets. Serious paranoia, understood.

Ralph responded to a burglary alarm in Kent Woodlands (an exclusive, wealthy enclave). It was routine, until a Vietnamese gardener was encountered. GOOK! Kill the bastard, now! He checked himself, and I didn't have to initiate an inquiry.

Ralph enjoyed his Harley low-rider, horses and his cherished Jaguar 12-cylinder coupe.

87

His new wife, Vicki, called me at the main office with a request: Could I meet Ralph at Marin General Hospital? He'd been out riding his horse, without a protective helmet, when a bee had stung his mount. Ralph had been bucked off and struck his head, ringing his bell pretty darned good. I had other priorities going on at the time and dispatched the local beat Deputy.

Ralph died that day; the horse was destroyed later. Damn! Another good man gone.

Why do we do what we do?

# Rookie Suicide Investigator

The young Deputy had just handled his first gory suicide, a gunshot to the head—his brains splattered around. Been there myself, several times.

He, I and a couple of other guys were having lunch afterwards and Rookie was regaling them, unnecessarily, with the tale and how well he handled it. His boasting finally got to veteran Deputy Art W.

Art went into the kitchen and returned with a small piece of raw liver and, from behind, surreptitiously placed it on Rookie's shoulder. A few minutes later, Art reached over from across the table and plucked it off, carefully examining it for the benefit of the others (and to the chagrin of Rookie). "You must have been very close to him," he mused. Art succulently ate it.

Rookie puked all over his plate. No more self-aggrandizing. Lesson learned. It takes time to learn the job and to keep the "bad stuff" to ourselves, regardless of the emotional expense.

Art died young of a massive heart attack. Not long before, he'd given a ride to a young man who pulled a knife on him and demanded his money. Art tried to tell him he was making a big mistake. The kid wouldn't give it up and ended up with two .38's. in his heart.

* * *

So why do I share this? So you might understand what we who serve you do. We pay a price, but that's okay—our choice. And that's why we drink, have failed relationships, commit suicide after our usefulness to our society seemingly has been utilized. Hope you understand. Those of us who are resourceful find other sources of inspiration and healing. Mine, at this time, is sharing my experiences and thoughts; riding my

Harley with my loving lady-friend, Irene; practicing Qi Gong and getting in the wind on the Tall Ship Hawaiian Chieftain!

Whatever works.

# Broken-legged Steve

Deputy Steve had a chemical imbalance in his body. He lived on a sailboat in Sausalito and once in a while when he was off his meds, he'd go over the edge.

He loved his job—keeping the peace; bad guys to jail, victims and survivors cared for, looking after the homeless and the down-'n'-outers, the hookers working the streets of Southern Marin, kids on the wrong paths. Just another guy with a badge, a gun and a big heart.

A bad guy kicked his knee out of its socket down in Bolinas one night. Screwed him up, physically and emotionally. Couldn't work any more, even after a few operations. Takes only three pounds pressure to do it, if one does it right. Did it to my brother once, by accident, when we were horsing around. I later perfected it in a martial arts class.

He did some other things, trying to make a go of it, but it broke his spirit not to be out there pushing around a patrol car or walking in dark places, taking care of business. Kind of like trying to shift gears without using a clutch, grinding up the teeth in the transmission.

Thanksgiving Day at his folk's house he made a statement. Steve left a very detailed, lucid six-page letter on his father's desk. It was hard to read through his pain and to grasp his rationale—must have been a bear to write it. Steve blew out his brains in the back yard while family was gathered upstairs for the traditional dinner. The pyracantha bushes were laden with their scarlet and orange holiday berries to attract and intoxicate song birds. Juxtaposition can be a mockery of life.

Why did he do it? Why the way he did? He tried to tell us but our ears and brains were as dysfunctional as he was. I miss him . . .

We all do what we have to do.

# The Judge

Coming home, late at night, around 12:30 after a swing shift at the jail, my wife at the time, Susan, was driving our top-heavy Volkswagen Westphalia camper. This idiotic, drunk person, driving an official unmarked Sonoma County vehicle with a Sheriff's Office radio, thought he was on the (Russian) River Road in Guerneville, the next county north, trying to get home. He was coming head-on in our lane on narrow and twisting Lucas Valley Road.

I told Susan to get off the road. We ran up an embankment and fortunately did not overturn.

I got in the driver's seat and pursued him and eventually got him to pull over by flashing the high-beam headlights. He was so drunk that he not only did not know where he was, he could barely stand unassisted.

He said, "Relax, Sonny Boy, I'm a Judge" and flashed a large gold badge.

I honor and respect those of us in our profession who protect our citizenry and compassionately interpret the law, but this man was out of control, a loose cannon rolling across an old-time sailing vessel's deck, no comprehension of the consequences of irresponsible behavior.

I cannot be judgmental—We all have paths through our lives; some good, some not too comfortable. We learn, we share with others for whom we care. Then we reach out to others unknown to us as individuals but who may make a positive difference in global harmony.

I gave The Judge two choices: I would arrest and book him in the Marin County Jail or I would detain him in our home in rural Nicasio. He chose the latter. We made a large pot of coffee and talked through the night. He raised Clydesdale horses, some of which he sold to the Budweiser team.

I telephoned my Undersheriff, Sid Stinson, and told him what was happening. He was on Valium due to extreme pain in his back, but I felt it was necessary to advise him. He called back the next morning to confirm what I had told him. He was somewhat incredulous . . . but assured me that it was okay.

Around four in the morning, The Judge decided to leave. I blocked his way, telling him he was not yet ready to go. He looked at me in a questioning, challenging way, then realized I was serious. He sat down again. He knew of that which I spoke.

How is it that some people connect and others don't? I don't know. Trust your instincts.

At seven, I allowed him to leave, then called him in his chambers at nine o'clock as he was ready to go on the bench. He seemed okay, incredibly.

He died several months later. He was highly talented, but wasted his life through alcoholism, just as I have jeopardized my own.

I wish that I had known him earlier. Maybe I could have made a difference. I can't blame him, I can't blame myself—It would be a waste of energy.

Life goes on . . .

# Dead Blue Eyes

She was a pretty little Scandinavian gal of seventeen, with long, blond hair and eyes of azure; a tantalizing glint in her Daddy's proud eyes. She'd obviously "become of age" and Daddy probably deduced that she'd already given her virginity to some lucky boyfriend. He never suspected her of promiscuity. Now, she was energetically experimenting with her ripe sexuality, determined to learn the "ins and the outs" of the world's oldest profession. I'm guessing in hindsight that she could have become extremely successful as a high class call girl; perhaps even in the realms of Fetishism and/ or BDSM.

The local, lecherous and married banker cared little for the safety and well-being of his victim—only his own gratification.

So it was, one solitary night with his wife out of town, that Banker Boy was living out his fantasy—a beautiful blue-eyed young woman was laying in the family bathtub, naked, her gorgeously lithe body pulsing in anticipation, knowing her power over the married lecher. He lowered his weight over her and they played around for a while and kissed a bit, the water in the tub overflowing.

Then he took her slender neck in his beefy hands and slowly strangled the life from her as he gratified himself.

As she died there, eyes staring upward through the water toward the ceiling, she asked herself, "Why me, Lord, Why now? I haven't even made it to adulthood!"

Had he planned and plotted this murder? Was there a dark, unresolved conflict from his childhood? Or simply spontaneous, selfish insanity. Bastard!

I had no involvement in this case, but I know the details and have seen the photographs.

My friend, the investigating officer, is still haunted by the callous senselessness of it . . . so am I.

She was so pretty, just like my own daughter . . . her Daddy must know that we still care.

# Seven Kids and a 12-guage Shotgun

After the infamous Marin County Civic Center shoot-out on August 7th, 1970, and the uprising at San Quentin Prison in October of the following year, there were a lot of jumpy folks, talk about revenge killings by the bad guys, with Judges, cops and, in particular, a wealthy doctor who lived with his family on a 700 acre ranch in Nicasio. He had the unfortunate distinction of being on a hit list for having tried unsuccessfully to save the life of a San Quentin inmate.

In the middle of the night, he packed up his family and left without a trace that I knew of. There were whispers about Australia and South Africa. I was in a trusted position, with some pretty good connections I thought, but the F. B. I. and even Interpol wasn't talking to me. I still don't know the end of this chapter.

What I do recall, vividly, is that after putting in my usual long day, I was tasked with protecting the family of Judge Peter Allen Smith. I took a quick shower, threw on a clean uniform shirt, inserted fresh batteries in my 4-cell Kel-light, reconnoitered his neighborhood and the nooks and crannies of his Kentfield Gardens home. He is a good Catholic man, and he and his wife had seven children to prove it. They couldn't understand why there was a stocking-footed deputy snoozing fitfully on their living room sofa, his ears tuned to the slightest creak in the floor, a Remington 870 loaded with double-ought buckshot cradled in his arms, when they awoke for strawberry pancakes the next morning. They were the best pancakes I'd had in a long time.

Judge Smith is now 91, still plays tennis once a week and has lunch with other judges monthly.

Some gory grit that also come to mind: Officer Diamond feigned death while "they" were clipping away at his carotid artery with some nail-snips. He later testified against them. Smokey and "Stew" were there. Thompson .45 slugs everywhere. So also was there a lot of blood. I'm thankful that I wasn't part of that episode, but I identify.

Steven B. and Angela D.—don't believe for a second that won't be held accountable when the Day of Reckoning comes.

Officer "K" was the father of an accomplished lover later on. He died there, in the commingled blood. She still hurts from the memory of him and her Mom, both alcoholics.

# Maggie, the Principled Prostitute

"The Mob" ran her out of the Las Vegas casinos. Eighteen-years-old, she'd been working solo, without a pimp, and not "paying her dues." Death or vicious assault at her age, she determined, would not be in her cards. Marin County was her haven, and so she returned. Soon, she had a baby son to raise.

Desperately poor yet resourceful, she embezzled from the welfare system, to the tune of $18,000. She didn't cover her tracks very well and was arrested. She plead "guilty" and was sentenced to many weekends at the Marin County Jail, affectionately referred to as the Blue Roof Inn. It is part of the only governmental complex designed by the late, famed architect Frank Lloyd Wright.

After the infamous Marin County Shoot-out in August of 1970 at the same complex, I was appointed Sergeant and, after three years in the newly created Security Division, was assigned to the Jail for an unprecedented five years. "The Brass" couldn't abide my independence and innovative techniques, such as barbering inmates while gaining jail house intelligence information, hence my "punishment."

Maggi would show up well before her scheduled check-in time. I could not help but notice her enticingly voluptuous form, nor her quiet serenity. Her voice was soft and well modulated, with the hint of a foreign accent. We chatted on a few occasions and I noted her firm conviction that she was not only repentant but determined to right her wrongdoings.

She was on Probation for five years but, paying off her debt at $50 a month would only modestly satisfy her obligation. She unnecessarily continued payments for many more years, until her moral obligation was satisfied fully, because it was the right thing to do.

Cops (and their spouses) have a tough row to hoe. They are committed to making our home environments safer places to live, sometimes not knowing the impending costs of their passions. Alcoholism, divorce and suicide are rampant. Sexual dalliances abound. My first wife and I were separated and divorce was imminent. Sexual tension was released all too often alone and without the warmth of another human being. In other words, I was horny as a pet raccoon.

Maggi and I met at her apartment after swing shift one evening, sipping Tequila for a while then, inevitably, slipping off to her bed. Her well trained Kegel muscles were a milking machine. I went home the next morning, a happily drained and satiated man! Our occasional intimate friendship would prove to be life-bound.

Many years later, my second marriage was crumbling on the rocks of a rugged shoreline. We struggled to avoid a total shipwreck. It happened anyway.

Both of my former wives had many fine qualities: dedication to family and tolerantly accepting the demands and risks of my profession. I loved them deeply in different ways— and they truly loved me. My sexual appetite and proclivity for experimentation and enhancement most likely were the primary destructive elements. I did not want to miss anything in this one-time go-'round life of mine. Some would think of me as a lying, cheating and unprincipled bastard. I prefer, and am more inclined and comfortable with, equating it to the not unnatural order of our kind.

I was now back on the streets as a Patrol Sergeant, finally. Monthly training gave us a break from the routine, albeit occasional fright, of Patrol or Jail House conflict. We get accustomed, sometimes addicted, to the rush of adrenaline that accompanies danger.

Maggi gratefully received my suggestion to rendezvous during my long lunch break. Her husband, while being an attentive father, was not much of a provider nor, apparently, was he an imaginative lover. Maybe it's just my healthy ego talking to me.

A graciously served light brunch was followed by Maggi's demure disclosure that she was at the heaviest peak of her menstrual cycle and that our pending intimacy would be somewhat messy. To my then poorly informed awareness, Maggi also disclosed frankly that her sexual appetite was always at its height at these times.

Encouraged by my curiosity and reaction, she tucked her young son down for a nap and covered the bird cage. Mindful of my limited time, we retired to the bedroom, hastily undressed each other; then I enthusiastically jumped her nicely cushioned bones and bountiful breasts! Ecstasy for us both!

I returned to the afternoon training session late, reeking of her essence. Did my classmates sense my euphoria from my "Cheshire Cat" grin? It was one of the best afternoons of my life!

Throughout the next couple of decades, she raised her son in the best schools she could afford, encouraging him to make something of himself, as did I. She acquired a teaching certificate and utilizes it to this day. Eventually she married her current husband, a match that seems well made. He knows nothing of any of this, and that is the way it will remain.

It is no coincidence that "Maggi" is my Mary Magdalene, the soiled dove of Biblical fame. I'm no Jesus, but I have been instrumental in Maggi's life, as she has been in mine.

I admire her greatly. We continue our platonic relationship to this day.

A bit of advice: if you can't salvage a marriage, at least keep and nurture your close and/or intimate friends. They just might be there when you need them the most—or when they might need you.

# Graveyard Shift ~ My Son Dies

It was a routine night, reporting at the Marin County Civic Center as one of two Sergeants for the Graveyard Shift (midnight 'til 8:00 AM) My counterpart, Al "Stew," Stewart, was down in Marin City, our bastion of racial diversity in the Southern part of the county, close to the Golden Gate Bridge. I'd shined my boots and polished my badge and brass accouterments on my Sam Browne belt as I was mentally concocting my normally low-key but high expectancy briefing.

The off-going Sergeant, Wade Powell, took me aside and told me quietly that my wife, Susan, had had a medical emergency and was on the way to the hospital in San Rafael. We were expecting our first child after a whole lot of fertility testing and many disappointments and false pregnancies. I called home. She had lost a lot of blood from what we learned later was a "spontaneous abruption" where a broken blood vessel causes the placenta to separate from the uterine wall and precipitates premature birth. Her Mom had come over right away. Susan was quietly self-assured, as many women are when challenged. She even took the time to remove the Christmas tree ornaments, which had been her earlier intention to while away the hours we were apart. Men are pussycats of courage, by comparison, usually.

For some crazy reason, I figured that my primary responsibility was to my Deputies, to get them on the road with sage words of advice that would ensure their survival and effectiveness for the next eight hours. I was clearly confused, most likely in a form of shock.

Rich Laden, one of my Viet-Nam War unsung hero Deputies, was incredulous. "Weldon, what are you thinking? We can handle it—you belong with your wife. Get the Hell over there where you belong." Right!

I pushed the old Volkswagen camper as hard as I could, fearing it might blow her little engine, over the Golden Gate

Bridge to Kaiser Hospital in San Francisco. Susan and her ambulance crew had been diverted there, after the local hospital determined that they could not adequately deal with her life-threatening condition.

I knew early on that I would be present at the birth of my child, and had decided that, if necessary, I would handcuff myself to my wife in order to overcome any resistance by hospital personnel. Now the test came.

The anesthesiologist was a bitch. I could see her disdain and uncomfortableness for me being a father in the "delivery room" as she readied her station for an emergency Caesarean-section operation. She screwed it up, big time. Susan felt the excruciating pain and heard the urgent instructions as they sliced open her belly. "Give her something to loosen her up," she heard. She couldn't respond in any way, not even to squeeze her hand in mine. Later, all of the hospital staff in attendance became aware and were shocked and humbled at their errors. Life is not just, sometimes.

The young surgeon-pediatrician strongly resembled Prince Valiant of Sunday funnies lore—handsome, chiseled features, shiny black hair in a bob. He lived an alternative lifestyle on a houseboat in Sausalito. He understood my desire and determination and had no reservations about my presence. I scrubbed up and donned the headcover, gown and booties, then joined my wife as she approached Death's Door. Nobody ever prepared me for this . . . and it was happening fast.

Adam was pulled out of the gaping slash and immediately perforated with multiple IV's. He winced a few times, then settled into the routine. The damned flatline alarm kept going off as the doctor discussed the status with me. Finally, the nurses got him over to Adam's inert tiny body. His lungs had not fully developed. He died in a bit, was gone forever, except in spirit and my memory. I died a little bit with him.

Each night, after spending hours with Susan at the hospital, walking past the morgue, I would drive home with my feelings welling up. At home, I bellowed, I shouted, I sobbed and heaved great shudders and let the tears rinse my gut and my face.

Damn it! Why me, Lord? Why have you challenged me so much?

Adam Zebediah Marvin-Travis had a purpose in his very brief life on this Earth. He accomplished it well. He taught me that one brief shining light can illuminate the way for others to see the way to assist their fellow man in times of disappointment and great loss. I have periodically and gratefully used his lesson to assist others . . . and I am blessed by his brief presence in my life.

"He came to us too early. He tried his best but didn't have enough of a chance. He had curly blond hair, a slender physique and piano-playing fingers. He will always be a part of me."

# Final Solution by a Deputy

Deputy Al was senior to me by about four years. He was what I would call a yeoman sort of officer . . . he did his job competently and had no great aspirations to be promoted. He came to work, did what had to be done and went home. I knew that I would surpass his career, most likely becoming his Sergeant one day.

We didn't know that "home" for him was not the rewarding place it used to be. He enjoyed his kids but, apparently, the sexual fire that had annealed his marriage early on burned no more.

Some of us noted his increasing disconnectedness while on Patrol and wondered what was going on with him. Al dismissed my one query if everything was okay—I guess he didn't trust me enough to talk freely. Shortly, he accepted a position within our Civil Division—serving subpoenas, wage garnishments, eviction notices and such. Maybe the Brass thought he shouldn't be making the critical decisions necessary to our duties while on Patrol.

There came a day when Al met an attractive woman at her front door to serve her a paper. Abruptly and without any enticing provocation from the lady, he grabbed her breast and started fondling her. Then there was the disclosure that this was not the first such incident.

The Brass placed him on "Administrative Leave" and arranged for private psychiatric counseling. Every workday morning, he would suit up at home and drive away. His wife didn't have a clue, did not know what had occurred—that she bore some responsibility or that Al was no longer doing his job as a cop and not attending to his deteriorating mental health. He'd just stay out and about, not keeping his appointments, then would return home at his "end of shift."

One morning, as he sat in his car in front of their home, he blew his brains out. I wish I'd known how bad it was—I might have prevented it.

# Barbecued Oysters at the Roadblock

Charlie Johnson raised oysters in Drake's Estero, off Sir Francis Drake Blvd., beyond Inverness with his Philippina wife and extended family. In fact, he pioneered in the USA the Japanese method of suspending the bi-valves from hemp lines so they would have better access to the sea nutrients. He grew them large and not-so-large, plump, juicy and tasty, like a fine Italian woman past her presumed prime, whom any philogynist would appreciate.

During **The Flood of '82**, fourteen inches of huge raindrops fell in the first 24 hours and the entire Point Reyes Peninsula was isolated, each of the nine communities from its neighbors, due to land slides along Sir Francis Drake Blvd. and Highway One. As time wore on, we were worried about looters from "over-the-Hill" and the inquisitives getting in the way of the National Guard engineers and the "CCC-ers" (California Conservation Corps workers). We even had opportunistic and greedy scavengers coming over from the East Bay to shamelessly take advantage of meal and lodging chits being handed out by the Red Cross.

Susan and I, together with my 12-year-old Zachary and our 2-year-old Katrina, were caretaking the old Marconi Cove property midway up the East side of Tomales Bay after it had been sold by the infamous Synanon Foundation, the drug rehabilitation organization that went **really** sour after initial success. Also on the 29-acre facility were another couple (the local pharmacist and his writer lady-friend) and a "self-repatriated" bachelor, a former Synanon member who still shaved his head and who took care of all the mechanical stuff, like maintaining the fresh water and sewage treatment plants, fixing broken windows, mowing the lawns with a large tractor.

Day #4 of The Flood, we went from two couples, four kids, one weird bachelor and a mischievous poltergeist

106

to maybe 350 folks and 150 pieces of heavy, military earth-moving equipment—10-wheel, all-wheel-drive dump trucks that could wade through water five feet deep. Our home, "Bayview," became the evening Command Post after we'd had dinner down at the "Inn." The honchos from the Guard and CCC with some of their key people would sit around our living room, drinking bourbon neat or on the rocks, strategizing for the next day. We had the living quarters, the commercial kitchen, fourteen cords of seasoned, split firewood, plenty of parking, three fire trucks, a five-bay service garage. We had only three phone lines and a very limited supply of natural gas. Woody from the phone company and De Carli's Butane Gas fixed us up real fine in short order.

It was a marked improvement over the muddy Guardsmen staying five to a room at Barnaby's-by-the-Bay in Inverness and the CCC-ers commuting 25 or 30 rough miles from San Rafael. We were also putting up about twenty-five locals who had been washed out and another thirty or so Quakers who had come in from out-of-state to quietly lend a hand.

We were coping, doing it, making it happen. We were running on fumes, in both senses. We got pretty creative and just a tad silly around eleven, but I won't tell you where we got some of our supplies or who was sleeping with whom.

Two people among our guests had already gone crazy: one was the co-chef for the Guard, who resented and couldn't handle sharing the kitchen with the Conservation Corps and who missed his family with a terrible, sick compulsion; the other was a young girl with the CCC, which often took in unstable kids at risk. She lost it when she was caught stealing and faced expulsion from the Corps.

Charlie thought it would be a nice break, along about day #10, for everybody to relax a bit, sit down together and enjoy some of his famous barbecued oysters, heated and treated as only Gonzalvo could do them with his secret combination of sauces.

We set it up for early Saturday evening and Charlie, true to his 80-year-old-word, personally delivered **fourteen bushels** of just-plucked **large** oysters. And that was just the appetizer! There was one 17-year-old kid from Kansas who previously had no idea what one was. He gulped down, at last count, seven plates-full, three and four to a plate. Last I saw him, he was waddling around like a self-satisfied and bloated sow, only with a silly grin on his face, trying to keep the contents of his belly from erupting.

Oysters don't keep very well for very long and we didn't want them to go to waste. What to do with the leftovers? I didn't care . . . I was too exhausted and still had to make one final round of the hardest-hit areas before I turned in. I tossed down a double shot of Ancient Age and hit the road again. It was pretty much deserted, pitch black except for my headlights. I was very lonely and felt the weight and safety of the entire community on my shoulders.

Next morning, along about 10:30 after changing of the guard at seven, I tooled over towards Inverness Park. At the intersection of Bear Valley Road and Sir Francis Drake Blvd. stood my fearless, if **somewhat** unorthodox Lieutenant, Art Disterheft (on the right) and Deputy Skip Richardson, by one of the garbage can fires that we kept burning with storm debris and seasoned oak from Synanon. They'd scrounged the top of a barbeque grill somewhere and were having a breakfast of the left-over oysters al dente, sharing with anyone who came along. It wasn't quite the Hangtown Fry with added bacon pieces and hash brown potatoes that you could get at The Station House, but it sure warmed the spirit . . .

# 10-7 O/D, forever, sort of

Alvin was a very unusual, strange, frightening, potentially dangerous man. He was very dark black, well-muscled and with a perpetual scowl on his heavily typical Negroid features. Sometimes he appeared to be a gentle genie, tender, playful, full of wonderment, almost child-like, and the scowl would be gone. Other times, he'd scare the bejezus out of anyone who ventured too close.

He was highly skilled in the martial arts, in particular with the associated weapons: shuriken ("throwing stars,"); ninchukas ("nunchucks") derived from flails used to separate grain from chaff—I have my great-grandfather's; swords (the long one is a "daito" or "katana—the shorter one a "wakazashi;" the wooden practice ones are called "bakkan" and are sometimes used as longer batons by modern-day mounted police. Another unique defensive weapon is the "sai" which is a short, handheld, soft metal Neptune's trident of sorts. It was used to intercept and break sword blades, utilizing a sharp twisting movement. I can't swear to the accuracy of these terms, or that Alvin was skilled in all of them, but you get the general idea.

When the family was living in the predominantly black community of Marin City, I heard of him fatally shooting a running dog with an arrow at a considerable distance.

Later, he lived with his genteel Mom in "Lower Sc'bow" as we sometimes disparagingly referred to the flood-prone Santa Venetia neighborhood near the Civic Center. There were some mighty fine and stable families living in this lower cost neighborhood, but it also contained a good helping of low-lifes and assorted crooks.

We'd had numerous calls about his strange behavior over several years. He'd jump out of bushes, dressed in flamboyant robes and a turban over his shaven head, to frighten children on their way home from school; sometimes, his "victims" were adults walking their dogs or otherwise just going about their business. We learned, too, that he had jars of his own urine to drink; that he had broken numerous 2x4 studs in the home's walls with his bare hands.

One Graveyard shift, he'd been acting up at home, and his mother had asked for help. Deputies Rich S. and Glen G. responded, backed up by my friend, Sergeant Rich Laden. Rich had seen some heavy action as a LLRP ("Lurp"—Long Range Reconnaissance Patrol) Ranger in Viet Nam so he was no stranger to pending death. They encountered Alvin coming down the hallway of the little bungalow. He approached them in a menacing manner; wearing his typical turban; a sword in his waistband; carrying spears in both hands; a fork clenched in his teeth. The guys didn't see the "Bowie"-type knife tucked in his waistband.

All three men had their guns drawn as they ordered him to stop and drop the spears. He whipped out the big knife and, with the swiftness of a viper, it twanged into the floor between the two deputies. Rich wrote me recently, "I do not know why nobody fired their weapons . . . we all were drawn on him." All three rushed and subdued him; confiscated all of his weapons and took him off to the Blue Roof Inn. The impressive array of exotic weapons greeted me in the Squad Room the next morning as Rich filled me in.

Over the years, Alvin came under the supervision of the Probation Department which saw to it that he received proper medical care, including oral or intravenous dosages of calming and stabilizing drugs. When he was on his meds, he was quite mellow and would walk with what we call the "Thorazine Shuffle." When he was off, when he wasn't shuffling, we worried; and knew we would have to deal with him once again.

On the last day of my full-time employment, a dayshift, I made the usual rounds of three of the four substations (Marin City had its own Sergeant, as usual), picking up reports, delivering station mail—routine stuff, except I made it a point to see *all* of the on-duty Deputies that day to say my fare-thee-

111

wells. Around 3:25, I pulled into the Sergeant's parking space under the arch of the Civic Center's Hall of Justice, gathered up my "stuff," picked up the mike and told the dispatcher, "This is 1X25, going 10-7 O/D at 4-5-Forever"! Ten-seven means "out-of-service; O/D means "off-duty;" "4-5" was the Main Office, first at the old court house in San Rafael, then at the newer Hall of Justice. "4-5" was the telephone number "way back when," long before my time, but still in use today. There was a short pause, then "10-4, 1X25 . . . Enjoy." There were a few nice echoes.

Then it came: "1Q31" (the dayshift beat officer in that section of the County) "respond to such-and-such a location. Alvin's acting up again. I was closer than the Deputy and it was at least a two-man detail. I said to myself, "DAMN! I hope I still get to retire . . ." and started to roll. Deputy G. arrived shortly after I pulled up to Alvin. We "triangled" him and the female deputy (who had a good rapport with him) said, C'mon, Alvin—time to go get your shot. "Okay, Missy G, I guess you're right." And off they went to the clinic. I exhaled a breath of relief and returned to the Civic Center to *really* go O/D.

# Remarkable Rendezvous of Old Cops Rough and Ready, Nevada County, California

I retired in '92, '94 and finally for good in '96 after 33 years but, like an old firehorse, when the bell rings, I'm still ready to go—always packing my Smith & Wesson 9mm. 15-round auto or, on occasion, my Colt .44-40 single-action Frontier Six-Shooter. The local boys on both sides of the law are beginning to know and appreciate me.

In November of 2009, some of us gathered for Ken Irving's final 10-7 O.D. at the Rancho Nicasio (Marin), near where he was raised as part of a pioneering ranching family, and where he spent virtually his entire life. Ken was a legend in our Department, my mentor, friend and a highly respected lawman in the greater enforcement community, which I prefer to refer to as the *Keepers of the Peace.*

One of Ken's more notable investigations was written up in *True Detective.* The Zimmermans, an older ranching couple who had befriended and graciously assisted their killer, were murdered by the young bastard who rode a 10-speed bike from San Anselmo, maybe 30 miles distant, out to their spread West of Novato.

He snuck into their bedroom as they were sleeping and, with a 4x4 leg of an oak table, brutally crushed their skulls. It was a bloody mess.

With his amazing recall ability and typical tenacity, Ken traced the bike, which had been discarded in a dumpster, back to the suspect, who was eventually arrested and convicted.

The *Fruit Jar Pickers,* a down-home gang of rough-hewn but talented musicians, play every Sunday at the Picker Palace, an abandoned gas station next to the blacksmith shop in Rough and Ready. A copper friend from out of my past, Jerry Brooks, dropped in. I had known him as a tall, handsome, dark-

113

haired Highway Patrol Motorcycle Officer—all spit and polish and a real gentleman to boot. He'd let me slide once, when he could have, should have arrested me for D.U.I. He's now gray, but still erect. His buddy set him up for me and I got the drop on him, good! I hornswaggled him for a bit, then got into some serious reminiscing. Eventually, he and his wife came home with us, unloaded a trailer of fire wood and continued our palaver.

That firewood was a gift from Ol' Bill Wilhelm, my 88-year old woodchucking buddy, who strums a guitar at the Picker Palace. He also is an 18 year veteran motorcycle officer of L.A.P.D. who lost three partners in gun battles and wrote a book of his exploits and experiences, *Code Two 'n' a Half.*

I ran the swing or graveyard shifts at the old Jail in the Blue Roof Inn for a five-year stint. When Jerry would arrive with a booking, usually a drunk driver, Deputy Bertie G., with her long, flowing red hair, fair complexion and Oklahoma Cherokee blood, would get all flustered and blush out when I alerted her to Jerry's arrival. She'd check her hair, freshen her make-up, even undo the second button of her uniform blouse to better display here voluptuous curves. She wasn't much good for the rest of her shift, but that was okay—I understood her natural inclinations.

Bill Gleason, another new friend up here and fellow member of our local Model 'A' Ford club, actually put the collar on Charles Manson, the notorious patriarch of a "family" of vicious, senseless, bloodthirsty killers. Bill has been featured in three films about his extraordinary accomplishments in our chosen profession. He is a quiet, unassuming man, but stays active as a volunteer investigator with the National Center for Missing and Exploited Children. He has been notably effective in that role.

As I enter into the autumn of my life, I ask you to learn from, reflect upon, and be thankful for your unsung local heroes who try their damndest to keep you safe.

**Pickers Palace & Fippin's Blacksmith Shop**

# Times Keep Rollin' On
## "Wild Bill" Wilhelm

I retired in from the Marin County Sheriff's Department '92, '94 and '96, (they just kept asking me back for special assignments, such as background investigations and as a Bailiff for high security court proceedings). Later on, I met a mighty fine and beautiful woman, "Serene Irene, My Bawdy House Queen," and we moved to Rough and Ready, up in the Gold County foothills and got hitched for life.

We became involved in all sorts of community activities—Chambers of Commerce; the local Grange; the rodeo committee (I used to ride bareback bronc in my young and carefree years); more recently the Law Enforcement and Fire Protection Council which benefits our Nevada County communities in ways not funded by taxes but by conscientious individuals and business owners who care. It's a small way by all of us to continue to assist those who appreciate us, and many others who don't.

One of my newer friends had a highly distinguished career as a motorcycle officer with the Los Angeles Police Department. Three of his partners were killed in gun battles. I've lost a few, too, but all were due to suicides. He was a bodyguard for Kenny Rogers, did a lot of movie work with one of his two Harleys, made to look like an "official" police motorcycle. Later on, up here in Nevada County, he lived on test pilot Chuck Yeager's ranch. He wrote a great book, *Code Two 'n' a Half*, about some of his experiences and exploits. It's a quick read.

In Marin County, I was in the thick of it with the Hell's Angels, the Gypsy Jokers, the Black Panthers, the Black Liberation Army, the Symbionese Liberation Army, the Weathermen Underground (Obama's friend and advisor, Bill Ayers along with his girlfriend, Bernadine Dohrn). Down south, Bill was involved with the Watt's Riots, among many other dangers.

For the last couple of years, I've been writing a column for a monthly local paper, the Penn Valley Courier, entitled **Rough and Ready Ramblin's** under my *nom de plume* of Capt. A. A. Townsend—Founder of Rough and Ready.

Below is my tribute in that newspaper to a fine gentleman and fellow "Keeper of the Peace."

# "Wild Bill" Wilhelm
# Lawman and Friend

There he wuz, sittin' by his lonely on the porch of the old Hotel, down hill a bit and on t'other side of the Toll Road from Fippin's Blacksmith Shop, strummin' his gitar, gazing off into the far yonder, and softly singing some sad ol' Blue Grass songs—"I'll Fly Away;" "In the Sweet Bye and Bye;" "Walk that Lonesome Valley;" and finally, "Will the Circle Stay Unbroken?"

What wuz going through his mind? I let him be for a long, long time, just a-watchin' and a-thinkin'.

He and I were lawmen, Brothers of the Badge, best buddies and had been involved in some wild 'n' crazy times and shoot-outs. We rode stirrup to stirrup, chopped wood together, commizserated on our difikulties and rejoysd in the plezurs our wimmenfolk provided.

He wuz a-getting' old and hiz legs were giving out, just like mine—too many years of being in the saddle, most likely, and being bucked off more than a few times. We always climbed back up on the saddle for one more ride on that kinky cayuse we call life.

I dragged up a rickety ol' chair, sayin' nothin'. He glanced at me and sang softly on. Pausing betwixt his melodies, he looked me in my eyes and right down into the deepest part of my soul.

He knew that I knew that he knew. He wuz a-sayin' "So long" and, a little while later, "Thanks for being my friend."

He checked out a few days later, leaving a big hole in my heart.

We celebrated his deparchur up at the Nevada City Elks Club. It was a low-falutin' barn-rayzin humdinger.

The Circle will always Stay Unbroke.

See you later up yonder, Bill.

---

He actually *did* come back shortly later, playing a couple of little tricks to remind us of him, like a mischievous, happy poltergeist.

# Epilogue
# Badge Brother Murdered

I never knew this brother. He was born twenty-four years later than I but we had much in common. Jim Mathiesen was an Officer of the Peace more than a Law Enforcement Officer. He died courageously, unarmed, trying to defuse a volatile confrontation between an ex-con (with a history of violence and domestic abuse) and one of the con's ex-girlfriends. She and her family had been friends of Jim's for many years.

Departmental records reflect that we have not had an officer killed in the line of duty in at least 140 years. Now, as I struggle with my emotions of loss, frustration and anger over a fatal failure of our legal system, I tell myself that, officially, I have been "out of the business" for fifteen years, even though I still maintain my contacts in Marin and our "retirement" home in the Gold Country hamlet of Rough And Ready. Many a time I have unobtrusively supported local officers who were in tenuous situations. As the old saw goes, "You can take the boy out of the country but you can't take the 'country' out of the boy." So it is with me. A sense of altruism pervades me and personifies my character, always backed up by a firearm, my martial arts training and relying on instincts honed by decades of dealing with hostile and unstable beings.

Jim's memorial service nearly filled the Marin Civic Center auditorium and was well covered by the local press and a Bay Area television crew. There was a bagpiper playing the traditional Amazing Grace and a recessionary; much pomp and circumstance; a constantly rotating Honor Guard with many departments participating; humorous anecdotes reflecting upon his zest for life; his wild dancing; his love of boating and high speeds; spontaneity; hard work ethic and hard partying; always being ready to lend a helping, encouraging hand.

It was strange being one of the oldest, but healthiest, retirees there.

Driving back home to our foothills, Irene and I did a lot of reflection upon the day's events. As the sun was setting, and after a long period of quietude, Irene softly said, "You're a lot like him." It is a compliment that I cherish.

# Memories of Being Fired & Reinstated

## ("The Naked Gun" [article by Jason Walsh] of 40 years ago is funny but with serious errors in it)

Wed., Oct. 9, 1968     San Francisco Chronicle   3

### Marin Dispute

# Deputy Is Fired For Nude Photo

A popular Marin county sheriff's deputy has been fired for allegedly posing in the nude as a photographer's model nine years ago.

He is Weldon C. Travis, 38, resident deputy sheriff for San Geronimo Valley.

The incident took place in 1960 while he was working his way through College of Marin and happened 4½ years before he joined the sheriff's department.

Travis is president of the Marin county Deputy Sheriffs Association.

**SILENT**

Sheriff Louis P. Mountanos refused to comment on last Friday's firing of Travis on the advice of county counsel Douglas J. Maloney.

Travis, likewise, declined to comment on the advice of his attorney, David R. Baty.

"We are going to fight the dismissal, which was based on acts that were neither illegal nor immoral and which occurred many years before Mr. Travis joined the sheriff's department," Baty said.

According to Baty, Sheriff Mountanous received from an anonymous source a copy of a "figure study magazine" containing a photograph of Travis.

**BACKGROUND**

The attorney quoted the sheriff as saying "this

WELDON C. TRAVIS
He'll fight dismissal

doesn't fit the image of a Marin deputy sheriff."

The photograph, Baty said, was published without the knowledge or consent of Travis.

Baty said Travis had been working at a service station to pay for his college education when he was approached by a photographer to pose in the nude for $5 an hour.

At that time, Baty said, Travis' parents knew he was working as a model and so did his girl friend, Mary Lou, who is now his wife.

Travis has ten days in which to demand a hearing before the Marin county Personnel Board.

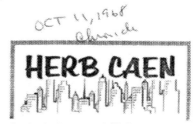

OCT. 11, 1968
Chronicle

# HERB CAEN

### Friday's Fractured Flicker

LET US TURN now to Marin Sheriff Louis Mountanos. Mountainous Lou made himself look faintly ridiculous a few days ago by firing a well-liked Deputy Sheriff who, while working his way through College of Marin years before, had posed in the nude as a photographer's model — and hold your "Horrors!" for a second, Tiger Thompson recalls that many years before all this, another impoverished student working his way through another school — in this case Stanford — earned some money by posing in the raw for art students. HIS name was Herbert Hoover.

    ★   ★   ★

News Item: "Marin county Sheriff Louis Mountanos has fired a deputy who posed for a nude photo long before beginning his law enforcement career."

# LETTERS TO THE EDITOR

# WHAT OUR READERS SAY

## Travis In Nude For Our Readers

Attached is a picture of Deputy Weldon Travis in the nude. It might be psychologically useful in pointing up the invalidity of his recent dismissal from the sheriff's department.

A caption on the front page might mention its release, but the picture might come as a joke on the page to which the reader is directed to find the rest of the article.

It seems obvious that the organized underworld is using this means of getting rid of him. I am surprised that their tactics are permitted to be successful to the extent that they have been.

RUTH TRAVIS
(Mother of
Weldon Travis)
WOODACRE

## Travis A Credit To County Police

For one reason or other I have had occasion to call the sheriff's office for help in the past few years. Officer (Weldon) Travis responded to the calls and conducted his duties with dispatch and courtesy. I felt he was a credit to the Marin County police force.

Were it not for people posing in the nude, the world would be without many of the great art masterpieces, Michelangelo's "David" for instance. The Christ figure in the "Pieta" is practically nude.

My four sons grew up in Marin County. They took whatever jobs turned up to help them through school and college. They washed dishes, worked in gas stations, helped carpenters, but I doubt if any of them would have had the intestinal fortitude to pose for an art class.

It is a grave sin to deprive a man of his good reputation and to take away his means of livelihood.

Very few of us have no skeletons in our closets so may I be trite in saying,

"Let him who is without sin cast the first stone."

MARGARET WHITELOCK
WOODACRE

Welden C. Travis posing in the nude

## Mountanos Bares Mind, Not Body

If your reporting is correct on the Deputy (Weldon C.) Travis incident, Sheriff Mountanos may never have posed nude but he is certainly baring himself to the public now.

I hope that our little Harper Valley doesn't lose a good man as a result.

Better cover up, sheriff, your mind is showing.

PAT GEIS
Woodacre

---

# REMEMBER WHEN?

## 10 YEARS AGO
Oct. 14, 1958

Juanita Muscoe, proprietor of a Sausalito restaurant, a walking advertisement for her own cooking at 212 pounds, started a campaign to take off 79 to 99 pounds in three months.

Lt. Gen. Charles D. Palmer, commander of the Sixth Army, disclosed that the Army might base a Hawk missile site in Marin, possibly in the Mount Tamalpais area.

## 20 YEARS AGO
Oct. 14, 1948

Work on the new $400,000 San Rafael-Richmond ferry pier off Point San Quentin was "off to a good start," according to Oliver Olson, ferry company president.

The Marin County Health Department marshalled its forces to inform every resident and school child of necessary precautions in the face of a polio epidemic.

## Frightening Aspect Of Travis Firing

The front page stories in the Oct. 7 and 8 Independent-Journal regarding the debased moral fibers of Deputy Sheriff Welden C. Travis has caused me great concern. It is frightening to think that a young man who has held a part-time job as a figure study or photographer's model may jeopardize his future job opportunities, no matter how distant. Many accredited colleges and universities offer courses in life drawing and photography where live models, draped and undraped are used. It is hard to conceive that all models for such classes are thereby forfeiting any opportunity for professional status where high moral character is a requirement.

If it is the desire of the Sheriff's Office to uphold the law, penalties should be imposed upon the magazine that published the photograph of Mr. Travis without his permission rather than upon Mr. Travis. . . .

It would be comforting to believe that all members of local law enforcement agencies are beyond reproach, but being human, they like the rest of us have a few skeletons in the closet that are better left undisturbed. It is hard to believe that such an incident which has no reflection on the integrity of Mr. Travis as an individual or as a deputy sheriff, could have raised such an issue.

For justice to prevail the county should withdraw all formal charges against Mr. Travis and reinstate him. . . .

HOLLIS HARDIN
Woodacre

(More letters on Page 27)

125

# BEHIND THE SUN

## The naked gun

*Marin aroused when mob thwarted by 'Big Boy' magazine's Mr. September*

BY JASON WALSH

It wasn't the long *arm* of the law that county residents were concerned about 40 years ago this week.

More than mere suspicion had been aroused throughout Marin in October of 1968 after the *Pacific Sun* broke the deftly titled story "Deputy Sheriff Fights for Job in Nude Photo Scandal."

According to *Sun* assistant editor Alice Yarish, the county personnel commission that week was deliberating the law-enforcement future of

A mid-'60s example of what used to be referred to as a 'fag mag.'

"handsome, crew-cut, pink-cheeked deputy sheriff" Weldon Travis who was showing more than his badge on the pages of such magazines as *Tomorrow's Man, Fair Fellows* and *Times Square Stud*. Weldon's woes began the prior month when local deputies, conducting a narcotics raid upon a San Geronimo Valley residence, were leafing through a suspect's magazine rack in search of drugs when a certain flamboyant publication delivered a surprising rise to one unnamed officer: "He picked up a copy of *Butch*, the nude fag mag," described Yarish, "flipped through it and stopped dead—there in the all-together was fellow officer Weldon Travis."

But Weldon knew a "raw" deal when he saw one and took the stand at the hearing in his own defense. (He was "neatly and fashionably attired," the *Sun* stressed.) Travis explained that the photos had been taken back in the late 1950s when he was a starving student at College of Marin; he was told at the time they would only be used in art classes and never gave his consent for their use in *Mr. Naked.* Travis became aware the photos had been pirated and shared throughout the gay porn industry sometime in 1966. "About two years ago a friend told me he had seen one," explained that week's cover model for both *Heavenly Bodies* and *Big Boy* magazines. But he took no action against the publishers for fear of the bad publicity. More than 500

Mike Peters

community members had signed a petition in defense of Deputy Travis, who had been literally and figuratively forced to "hand over his gun" under very embarrassing circumstances.

But Travis's excellence as an officer was not in question, argued Sheriff Louis P. Mountanos, who'd engineered Travis's dismissal. Rather, he was fired because "the indiscreet photos would cause the public to lose confidence in him," rendering the crime-fighting Adonis impotent in the eyes of county residents.

After all the evidence was laid bare, the commission voted 4-1 to put Travis back in uniform and he was once again allowed to unsheathe his firearm for the public good.

These days Travis, 70, resides in the Gold Country town of Rough and Ready; his law-enforcement and modeling careers behind him, Travis and his wife market Tahitian dietary drinks for horses on the equine circuit. He laughs when recalling all the hubba-hubba hullabaloo over his 1960s appearances on the pages of *Paisano* and *Golden Boys.*

But in all seriousness, Travis insists his firing was less due to the porn world than the underworld—in fact, he says, it was a mob job.

"The photos had been brought to Sheriff Mountanos's attention because I had been stepping on the toes of La Cosa Nostra," says the former battalion stallion. "I had made some significant investigations [into the mob], but [someone in the sheriff's office] had a direct friendship with a Tiburon police lieutenant who was a high-ranking member of La Cosa Nostra." But Weldon made it clear he knew about some "strange disappearances out of the evidence locker" and that they were "running whores from San Anselmo to Nevada." It seems they messed with the wrong *Paisano.* ◆

**40 years ago**

126

# I'm An Old Cowboy

You're never too old to learn
And never too young to teach.

Call or write me sometime!

(530) 432-8866
weldontravis@Juno.com